THE AMERICAN VIEW OF DEATH: ACCEPTANCE OR DENIAL?

THE AMERICAN VIEW OF DEATH: ACCEPTANCE OR DENIAL?

by

Richard G. Dumont

and

Dennis C. Foss

Schenkman Publishing Company, Inc.
Cambridge, Massachusetts

Distributed by General Learning Press

SCHENKMAN BOOKS ARE DISTRIBUTED BY:
General Learning Press
250 James Street
Morristown, New Jersey 07960

Copyright © 1972 Schenkman Publishing Company, Inc.
Cambridge, Massachusetts

Library of Congress Catalog Card Number:
Printed in the United States of America

CONTENTS

TO OUR PARENTS:
George and Elsie Dumont
and
Woody and Jean Foss

Preface

It is a rare occasion and a highly gratifying experience, both intellectually and emotionally, when the relationship between a teacher and a student transcends formal academic expectations, and both are thrust into a mutually challenging and exciting creative adventure. This book had it's genesis in such a fashion. It arose out of a thesis written by Dennis Foss when he was at Bates College, and since its inception, the authors have collaborated closely to elaborate, modify, and refine the ideas explicated within the original thesis.

This monograph has been written deliberately so as to be congenial to a heterogeneous audience. The topic is of obvious, timely, and ubiquitous concern and relevance, and it should therefore be of interest to the intelligent and thoughtful layman, as well as to the social scientist and the specialist in death research. We feel that the monograph's primary contributions are twofold. On the one hand, and specifically, it is intended to provide a clear articulation of and suggested resolution to the *acceptance-denial controversy*. On the other hand, and no less importantly, it contains a substantial and uniquely organized survey of the current state of social-scientific knowledge concerning American death attitudes. We leave it to the critical reader to judge the extent to which these objectives have been adequately met.

Our more or less exclusive focus upon death attitudes has compelled us to consider only indirectly such important aspects of death as funeral and burial customs, bereavement practices, and the like; for an application of the sociological imagination to death-related topics other than attitudes, the reader is referred to a more general text, such as Glenn M. Vernon's recent and important contribution to the literature, *Sociology of Death*.

We would like to express our most sincere appreciation to Professors George Fetter and Sawyer Sylvester of the Bates College Department of Sociology and Anthropology, Dr. and Mrs. Clarence Morris, Miss Frances Gormley, and Dr. Baheej Kleif for their careful reading and constructive criticism. Similarly, we are extremely grateful to Mr. Allan Crites and Dr. Thomas Conroy for providing us with certain references which would have not been otherwise available. Thomas Burnham, who typed the thesis, will be long remembered for his dedication and perseverance. Finally, our deepest thanks go to our wives, Pauline Dumont and Joyce Foss, for the immeasurable aid, comfort, encouragement, and inspiration they extended, and for doing whatever was necessary to expedite the completion of the manuscript, ranging from typing and proofing to making insightful and penetrating observations and suggestions.

Richard G. Dumont
Lewiston, Maine
and
Dennis C. Foss
Durham, New Hampshire

...I suspect that mortality has replaced sexuality as the obsession of our time.

T. George Harris, Editor
Psychology Today.

The Problem

Hora incerta, mors certa

Ubiquitous and ultimately inescapable, the phenomenon of death has always presented both a profound mystery and a crisis to the human species. Throughout time man has had to cope with the eventuality of his own death, and all cultures, even the most primitive, have dealt with death by evolving beliefs concerning its significance. Virtually universal among primitives has been the view of death as a crisis to be endured subsequent to entering a new status.[1] However, it seems that modern man, unlike his preliterate forebears, conceives of death as the "ultimate catastrophe"; although he "can understand infinity,... [he] must learn to live with the hard fact of his own finiteness."[2] Twentieth century man prides himself on his ability to control his world; while he has exhibited substantial mastery over his physical and social environments, he cannot control his own death. True, he is currently able to delay it and to reduce its misery, but all of his cleverness and ingenuity have thus far been of no avail in eliminating it.[3]

As catastrophe of catastrophes, death is rendered still more difficult for the twentieth century American by several characteristic features of modern existence. During the nineteenth century, it was extremely difficult for the average American to avoid coming into regular contact with death, for death rates were high, and the average life expectancy at mid-century could not have been much greater than half of what it is today.[4] It has been observed, for example, that childhood deaths were so frequent at that time that one could not find a prayer book that did not contain at least five or six poems about meeting lost children in heaven.[5] Man was thus in constant contact with death, and he was thereby compelled to recognize it as a natural and a very real phenomenon. Regular exposure also resulted in the genesis of somewhat uniform ways of handling death, so that death was, in effect, truly a pervasive part of life.

Demographic changes, particularly those ushered in by the advent of modern medicine, have drastically altered the nature of death in that it has become an event befalling, primarily the aged. For example, while 6% of Americans who died in 1967 were less than fifteen years old, 77% were over fifty-five, and only 17% were between the ages of fifteen and fifty-four.[6]

The increasing restriction of death to those individuals lacking financial or familial responsibilities has thus removed it from the mainstream of life; in fact, the average American experiences death in his family only once every twenty years. The vision of our own death is at best blurred by the fact that we so seldom witness the deaths of others. Under these circumstances, death tends to be conceived more as an abnormality and, concomitantly, it becomes more difficult to cope with. Death in the modern world world is yet further removed from us: while a greater total number of persons die, the quality of these deaths is significantly different.

> In quantitative terms, the 20th century seems more death-ridden than any other. Yet mass death is strangely impersonal; an 18th century hanging at Tyburn probably had more immediate impact on the watching crowd than the almost incomprehensible statistics of modern war and calculated terror have today.[7]

How is the modern American able to cope with his own death when the deaths he experiences are infrequent, highly impersonal, and viewed as virtually abnormal? It is tempting in this society to look to our technology as the panacea that will ultimately rid us of this ill of ills. We do so in vain, however, for while the average life expectancy (the average number of years actually lived by a population) has revealed a most remarkable increase during the last hundred years, the human life span (the theoretically possible maximum number of years lived under a set of ideal conditions) remains unchanged. Although some scientists speak seriously of an indefinite life span, the prospects for the immediate future hardly serve to relieve man of his present anxiety.[8] Man remains mortal in a context in which his mortality is apparently becoming increasingly difficult to bear.

Despite its changing nature, however, death continues to play an important role in American life. In the United States, where the importance of objects, events, or situations is often judged in monetary terms, death seems an integral part of the American scene. For example, it has been estimated that at mid-century we were spending more money on funerals and associated accessories than on all our hospitals and sanitariums.[9] Cemeteries have become such big business that a cemetery operator selling an acre of plots has a potential profit range of $14,000,000 to $150,000,000 for that single acre.[10] Furthermore, many other death-related industries flourish in this country, their services ranging from making tombstones to producing sympathy cards.

Death is important to Americans in non-monetary terms as well, for studies have demonstrated that it is a frequent topic of thought for most of us. For example, one early study found that the vast majority of

Americans think of death anywhere from "once a month" to "daily," and that the only time we apparently never think about death is "during, before or after sexual intercourse."[11]

Thoughts of death are not restricted to the conscious level for death frequently inhabits the unconscious due to the high degree to which we symbolize it. That the death symbol tends to elicit an unconscious emotional response, is brought out by a study conducted by Meissner. While his subjects made few conscious responses to death symbols, concealed written examinations and Galvanic skin tests revealed frequent unconscious reactions to symbolic stimuli.[12] Our high degree of symbolization is evidenced by the extremely wide range of death symbols which are capable of eliciting strong emotional responses. Some of the symbolic words and expressions include "bird," "journey," "candle burning out," "sleeping person," "statue," "across the bridge," "black," "thunder," "water," "stranger," and "thirteen," to name but a few.[13]

Given an appreciation of the importance of death in the lives of Americans, as well as an understanding of some of the problems of death which are unique to twentieth century Western man, a vital question arises as to how Americans view death. Knowing they are going to die, what attitudes towards death do Americans hold? This book addresses itself to this question.

An attitude may be defined as "a relatively enduring organization of beliefs [we would also include values and expectations] around an object or situation predisposing one to respond in a preferential manner."[14] An important component of this definition is the notion that an attitude predisposes one to act in a certain way; it is precisely this factor which dramatizes the importance of studying attitudes toward death. Our knowledge of death necessitates attitudes toward it; thus,

> We are mistaken to consider death as a purely biological event. The attitudes concerning it and its meaning for the individual serve as an important organizing principle in determining how he conducts himself in life.[15]

Our attitudes toward our individual deaths, then, affect not only the way we view death, but also the way in which we live our lives. If one views his death with horror, he may have considerable difficulty in mustering the courage necessary to cross a street in heavy traffic. If, on the other hand, death is conceived as a pleasurable and exciting experience, one may not hesitate to walk a tightrope or to go over Niagara Falls in a barrel. Furthermore, as at least one writer in the area of death research has suggested, the type of immortality we seek affects our behavior. If we seek biological immortality (through our children) or social immortality (through works or deeds that testify to our existence and that live on in the minds of others), our philosophy toward life may be *carpe diem...* sieze the day (live it up). On the other hand, if we seek a transcendental immortality (life hereafter), we may try to live a life of good deeds, so that we will be judged favorably after death by the supernatural forces.[16]

Despite the obvious importance of understanding people's attitudes toward death, empirical research in the area is not as yet very extensive. In fact, the social sciences have only recently ventured into death research. In 1930 the recognized pioneer in the field, T. D. Eliot, began his campaign to persuade his fellow social scientists to study scientifically man's relationship with death. In a wide variety of scholarly journals he urged others to join him in this project.[17] The following excerpt conveys the flavor of Eliot's message:

> Great souls have, to be sure, always pondered the problem of cessation of self, and have written great words into the human record. They have done so, however, as seers, poets, prophets, philosophers, novelists, biographers, not as scientists... It remains to apply modern techniques of case histories, group studies, and documentary analysis to the attitudes and actual behavior of people toward death.[18]

Pleas such as this one earned Eliot the cooperation and support of a substantial number of fellow social scientists. Nonetheless, the continuing paucity of work in the area is evidenced by the fact that the latest bibliography of material on the topic (1965) lists less than four hundred entries, a large proportion of which are quite recent.[19] Furthermore, most studies have focused on such topics as bereavement and funeral and burial customs; only a few of the most recent have been concerned primarily with investigating the attitudinal dimension.

A greater interest in attitudinal studies may be stimulated, however, by a fundamental and germinal controversy over whether the American attitude toward death is one of acceptance or denial. While we are generally interested in gaining an understanding of how Americans view death, we will be concerned primarily with what appears to be a basic and recurrent contradiction in death research. Specifically, while some authors advance evidence which either explicitly or implicitly supports the contention that Americans deny their deaths, others suggest that the attitude is one of acceptance. Although this "controversy" cannot be said to have matured or evolved to the point of generating opposing and clearly recognizable schools, it is no less real for not having been more explicitly stated in the literature or even clearly recognized by serious students of death research.

John W. Riley seems to imply his awareness of the *acceptance-denial controversy* in his discussion of the current status of social scientific knowledge on the subject of death. In citing Talcott Parsons' recent theoretical contribution, in which Parsons takes issue with advocates of the denial contention by arguing that acceptance is becoming the modal American view, Riley notes the indeterminacy of knowledge regarding

> ...a 'normal' or active orientation... and a deviant orientation that is essentially regressive and fatalistic. To the extent that this 'normal' orientation prevails in American society, the individual is expected to 'face up' to death in realistic terms... At the same time, the deviant orientation to death is also clearly in evidence, and to this Parsons relegates the denial of the reality of death, which some scholars have regarded as the modal American view...[20]

A plausible explanation for the apparent lack of attention to this issue is suggested by Ernest Nagel's discussion of the distinguishing characteristics of science *versus* common sense.[21] Nagel argues lucidly that, because of the limitations imposed by the lack of specificity and demonstrable validity of common sense arguments and terms, it is possible, and indeed frequent, for contradictory explanations or accepted facts to exist simultaneously and even unrecognized for prolonged periods of time. In contrast, Nagel points out, contradictions tend to be relatively short lived in science, due to the very role they play in the conduct of inquiry: The existence of contradictions in science functions to stimulate research which is directed toward resolving the logical incompatibilities.[22] It is our contention that the existence of an acceptance-denial controversy, as well as the fact that it has received little recognition to date, is at least partially explained by the fact that the area of death research shares many of the same general methodological problems as sociology as a whole.[23] That is, there is little doubt that the distinguishing problems concerning the structure of explanation, the significance of concepts, and the nature of evidence in the area of death research are sufficient to allow its characterization as a "prescientific" inquiry.[24]

As a first step in advancing an adequate description and attempted resolution of the acceptance-denial controversy, it is necessary to specify clearly what is intended by the concepts 'accept' and 'deny.' We base our definitions on semantical considerations derived from current usage. *Webster's New World Dictionary* informs us that 'to accept' is "to receive favorably, to approve, to agree to, to believe in."[25] Thus, if we say that a person accepts his death, we mean that he believes that he must die and perhaps even approves of the fact that he is going to die. Normally, we also expect that he behaves in accordance with this acceptance, for as we have already indicated, the notion of attitude incorporates a predisposition toward a certain type of compatible behavior. In direct opposition to 'to accept,' 'to deny' is "to declare [a statement] untrue; contradict, to refuse to accept as true or right, to refuse to recognize, repudiate."[26] Hence, if we say that a man denies his own death we mean that he refuses to believe that he will die, that he feels that it is untrue that he will, or perhaps simply refuses to recognize that he must, die.

Which of these two words most accurately describes the American's attitude toward his death? In our attempt to answer this question we will not be concerned with abnormal attitudes such as those of suicide cases or psychopaths, except for the way in which they might shed light, by contrast, on normal attitudes. Furthermore, we will not deal with the attitudes of non-American cultures, save to note their similarity or dissimilarity to American attitudes when it assists in understanding the American attitudes. The reader should further be cautioned that occasionally a reference may be cited which supports one side or the other in what we have labeled the "acceptance-denial controversy." It should not be concluded that, because the researcher's work has been used to support one side or the other of the dispute, he is necessarily a proponent of the implied position. In fact, symptomatic of the low degree of awareness and articulation of the controversy, the direct opposite may be true in certain cases. Citation of such material is necessary, however, if we are to shed as much light as possible on both sides of the issue.

In pursuing the objectives we have set forth, we have divided the book into three major parts. *Part I - Predispositions* deals with the major factors which are relevant in determining our attitudes toward our own deaths. In Chapter One, we inquire into the process of death attitude formation and change. In Chapter Two, we discuss intensively the two major emotional responses to our own deaths, the fear of death and the death wish, which derive importance from the crucial role they play in attitude formation. Chapters Three and Four in *Part II - The Acceptance-Denial Controversy* contain systematic examinations of the evidence and rationale of both sides of the controversy as to whether Americans accept or deny their own deaths. Finally, in *Part III - Toward a Suggested Resolution,* we approach the controversy in three different ways, with each of the three contributing additional insights as to why research has yielded such contradictory findings and how the controversy might be resolved. In Chapter Five, we review the numerous methodological problems which have contributed to the ambiguity and inconsistency of research on death attitudes. In Chapters Six and Seven, we assume the position that, to date, death attitude research has characteristically proceeded out of an erroneous assumption and a misformulation of the question. Specifically, we argue that a single and uniquely American attitude toward death simply does not exist. Furthermore, we contend that the question, "Do Americans accept or deny the reality of their own deaths?", is naively and improperly put, since there exists substantial evidence to indicate that the culture of the United States and individuals of this society *both* accept *and* deny death, simultaneously.

At this point, it should be apparent to the reader that a major objective of this monograph is to invalidate a key question which it poses. Indeed, the authors deem this strategy to be both desirable and necessary, since the history of science testifies to the fact that enlightened inquiry frequently proceeds by invalidating what has heretofore been accepted as a relevant question. Nowhere is this more evident in social science than in the now classic "nature vs. nurture" or "heredity vs. environment" controversy. A very great stride was made when social scientists ceased serious debate over which was most important in the determination of human behavior, recognized that *both* genetic endowment *and* environmental influence were quite relevant, and forsook a pointless and unproductive debate to focus serious research and theoretical endeavors in both areas. The analogy between the "nature vs. nurture" and the "acceptance vs. denial" questions should be immediately apparent. In any event, it is our sincere hope that the contents of the following pages will prove stimulating and remedial in their effects upon the ongoing process of death attitude research and theory construction. We turn immediately to the task at hand.

NOTES

1. J.W. Riley, Jr., "Death and Bereavement," *International Encyclopedia of the Social Sciences,* Vol. 4, 1968, p. 20.
2. D.C. McClelland, "The Harlequin Complex," in Robert White, (ed.), *The Study of Lives,* New York: Atherton Press, 1963, p. 95.
3. C.W. Wahl, "The Fear of Death," in Robert Fulton (ed.), *Death and Identity,* New York: John Wiley and Sons, Inc., 1965, p. 57.
4. For example, Taeuber and Taeuber estimate the average life expectancy for the United States at the beginning of the nineteenth century at about 35 years, while United Nations data on Massachusetts show estimates of 41.5 years for 1850 and 50.5 years for 1900. See C. Taeuber and I.B. Taeuber, *The Changing Population of the United States,* New York: John Wiley and Sons, Inc., 1958, pp. 269-272; and United Nations, *Population Bulletin No. 6,* New York: United Nations, Table IV. 1, 1962.
5. S. Cleghorn, "Changing Thoughts of Death," *Atlantic Monthly,* No. 132, 1923, p. 809.
6. *Vital Statistics of the United States, 1967,* Volume II - "Mortality," Part B, Washington, D.C.: National Center for Health Statistics, Table 7.3, 1969, p. 7-76.
7 "On Death as A Constant Companion," *Time Magazine,* November 12, 1965, p. 53.

8. *Ibid.,* p. 52.

9. W.M. Kephart, "Status After Death," *American Sociological Review,* 1950, 15, p. 636.

10. Compiled on the basis of figures provided by J. Mitford, *The American Way of Death,* New York: Simon and Schuster, 1963, pp. 124, 126, 127, 132, 133.

11. W. Bromberg and P. Schilder, "Death and Dying," *Psychoanalytic Review,* 1933, 20, pp. 154-155.

12. W.W. Meissner, "Affective Response to Psychoanalytic Death Symbols," *Journal of Abnormal and Social Psychology,* 1958, 56, pp. 298-299.

13. *Ibid.,* pp. 295-299.

14. M. Rokeach, *Beliefs, Attitudes and Values,* San Francisco: Jossey-Bass, Inc., 1968, p. 112.

15. H. Feifel, "Attitudes Toward Death in Some Normal and Mentally Ill Populations," in Herman Feifel (ed.), *The Meaning of Death,* New York: McGraw-Hill Book Company, Inc., 1959, pp. 114-130.

16. H. Feifel, "Death," *The Encyclopedia of Mental Health,* Vol. 2, 1963, p. 430.

17. The following are illustrative: T. D. Eliot, "The Adjustive Behavior of Bereaved Families: A New Field for Research," *Social Forces,* 1930, 8, pp. 543-549; T.D. Eliot, "Bereavement as a Problem for Family Research and Technique," *The Family,* 1930, 11, pp. 114-115; and T.D. Eliot, "A Step Toward the Social Psychology of Bereavement," *Journal of Abnormal and Social Psychology,* 1933, 27, pp. 380-390.

18. *Ibid.,* pp. 380-381.

19. R.A. Kalish, "Death and Bereavement: A Bibliography," *Journal of Human Relations,* 1965, 13, pp. 118-141.

20. Riley, *op. cit.,* p. 22.

21. E. Nagel, *The Structure of Science: Problems in the Logic of Scientific Explanation,* New York: Harcourt, Brace & World, Inc., 1961. Ch. 1.

22. *Ibid.*

23. Specific methodological problems of death research are considered in Chapter Five.

24. For a discussion concerning logical and empirical difficulties in the area of concept formation, for example, see R. G. Dumont and W. J. Wilson, "Aspects of Concept Formation, Explication, and Theory Construction in Sociology," *American Sociological Review,* 1967, 32, pp. 985-995; and W. J. Wilson and R. G. Dumont, "Rules of Correspondence and Sociological Concepts," *Sociology and Social Research,* 1968, 52, pp. 217-227.

25. *Webster's New World Dictionary – Comprehensive Reference Edition,* New York: The World Publishing Company, 1961.

26. *Ibid.*

PART ONE
PREDISPOSITIONS

Chapter One

Attitude Formation and
Attitude Change

In a society in which parents appear to strive to deal realistically with many of the former taboos of parent-child conversation, such as sexual matters and items of authority, the subject of death not only remains unspoken, but appears to be, by comparison, increasingly avoided and disguised.

Robert Fulton speaking of American parents.

Before we are able to undertake a meaningful and fruitful discussion of American attitudes toward death, we must acquire at least an elementary understanding of the way in which such attitudes develop and change, as well as of some of the more significant factors influencing that development and change. Attitude formation is, of course, a major substantive and methodological concern of both sociology and psychology. From voluminous research efforts in both areas of inquiry have come a wide variety of measurement techniques, conceptual models, and theoretical schema, but it is neither necessary nor within the scope of this book to consider them here. Rather, we intend to focus exclusively upon those factors which specifically concern death attitude formation. It is also important to emphasize at the outset that, while the accumulated evidence may allow us to generalize to a certain degree, death attitude formation constitutes a highly variable process. The sources of this variation are numerous and primarily due to the fact that death itself, "...is a multi-faceted symbol whose specific meaning depends on the nature and fortunes of the individual's development and cultural context."[1] Consequently, it would seem that one's attitude formation process may be almost as variable as his personal experiences.

Typically, our first contact with death comes quite early in life, between the ages of three and eight. This first encounter is ordinarily indirect and involves hearing about death from others. Individuals have reported a wide range of responses to this initial indirect contact, including " 'still-ness,' 'curiosity,' 'awe,' 'wonder,' 'unexplained mysterious feelings,' 'fear inspiring,' 'something different and baffling,' 'bewilderment,' 'being far away,' and 'mysterious because of importance.'"[2] As children, we also begin to learn of our own eventual deaths by what one author has called "social death."[3] This is the process by which we come to feel the meaning of death through the death of someone with whom we are emotionally involved, such as a sibling, close friend, or parent.

Having experienced these initial contacts, the child apparently begins to think about death rather frequently, usually in the form of fantasies. For example, when groups of children were asked to complete stories which began with no reference to death, approximately fifty percent of the subjects did make reference to it in completing the fantasies.[4] Not only do children fantasize about death frequently, but they, along with adolescents, have been found to exhibit emotional involvement with death.[5] There is a marked tendency in American society to assume that children have a happy life and that their emotions are neither strong nor well-developed. Death is an area, however, perhaps one of several, where emotions are persistent and highly potent.

The child's emotional involvement with death characteristically takes the form of fear of death. Interestingly, this fear is manifested in a line from the oldest known and most popular children's prayer: "If I should die before I wake..."[6] While the following chapter includes a substantial discussion of the fear of death, it should prove instructive at this juncture to consider briefly the way in which this fear develops in children.

Numerous explanations have been advanced for the development of the fear of death in children. Among them, fear of the corpse seems to play a particularly important role. The corpse's unnatural coldness, as well as its lack of movement and response, make the first contact with a dead body particularly unpleasant. The corpse must,indeed, appear quite frightening to the child, the way it lies motionless and rigid, made up unnaturally with cosmetics, the face having an unusual and changeless expression, and the skin exhibiting the characteristic death pallor. Furthermore, the entire situation tends to be fear provoking–the casket, relatives and friends in grief, the moaning, sobbing, and screaming. "The result is a 'total situation' that gives a feeling of strangeness, which if strong enough, is called fear."[7] Most of us have read about or been told about a variety of traumatic experiences involving the touching of a corpse. There have occasionally been adults at wakes or funerals who have thought it a fine parting gesture for one or several of the children present to touch, or even kiss, the corpse, despite the likely protestations of the child.[8] In view of these and other similar events involving children at funerals, it becomes more readily understandable why children tend to fear and avoid corpses.

An exceedingly wide variety of other causes for the fear of death have been cited, including: fear of retaliation, fear of aggression by others, infantile separation fears, conditions of physical restraint, the transition between the naivete of the child and the maturity of an adult, the disappointment and guilt concerning unfulfilled potential, fear of the unknown, fear of pain, extreme guilt about aggressive death wished upon others, influence of adults with morbid superstitions concerning death, intense emotional experiences at funerals, fear of the dark, a wish to return to the mother, fear of suffocation arising from breathing difficulties in early infancy, and, last but not least, masturbation guilt.[9] It is interesting to note that in our research we have not found a single writer who suggests that to a child whose life has just begun, death, *per se,* might just possibly be frightening. Presumably, this "obvious" explanation lacks the aura of mystery which makes psychoanalytic journals such good bedtime reading.

Although most available evidence on the subject indicates that children do fear death, the results of one study suggest that the fear of death in children is so rare as to be virtually nonexistent. According to the authors of this study, it is not death which children fear, but rather murder.[10] In light of the mounting evidence which supports the proposition that a fear of death does indeed exist in both children and adults, and in view of the lack of a rigorous methodology employed in the study in question, one finds the aforementioned conclusion quite unacceptable.[11] Furthermore, it seems quite reasonable to advance the hypothesis that, even if children do fear being murdered, such a fear would probably generalize to a fear of death itself. Although the violence of the murder would undoubtedly be frightening, one who is afraid of being murdered would in all probability also fear being painlessly and accidentally gassed in his sleep. It would seem, therefore, that the fear of death is inextricably bound up with the fear of being murdered.

As the emotional reactions to death develop, the child also begins to think about death; in response to these emotional reactions, then, his beliefs and attitudes begin to form. Cousinet hypothesizes that there are three stages in a child's death attitude formation: at first the child refuses to accept the idea of death; then he substitutes a severe, but curable, disease for death; and, finally, the concept of death is grasped and no longer found to be troublesome.[12] Anthony distinguished five steps of death attitude formation which progress from ignorance of the word to a clear definition in logical or biological terms.[13] More recently, Nagy's research findings led her to propose that up to age five the child has no definitive thoughts on death, it being conceived as sleep, departure, or the like. Between the ages of five and nine the child personifies death [that is, he (death) carries *bad* children away]. At age nine and thereafter death is seen as the cessation of bodily life and something "beyond" is recognized.[14] Despite minor disagreement as to the names of the stages and the exact age levels, there exists at least minimal consensus that the

child, through successive stages, passes from non-awareness of the existence of death to viewing it in "logical, causal, naturalistic terms."[15]

As to the precise role of the American family in the process of death
attitude formation, there is substantial evidence to indicate that American
parents characteristically do not discuss death with their children; when
they do, however, they ordinarily behave in such a fashion as to make the
child more confused and anxious. By and large, in the United States,

> Children are shut out from the two great mysteries of life: birth [sex] and
> death... Death is ordinarily mentioned in whispers and its accompanying ex-
> periences are made alien to the child.[16]

It occasionally happens that parents are almost forced to talk to their
child about death, as, for example, when a close relative dies, or when
the child stubbornly persists in asking questions about it. A likely parental
response in these situations, after much hemming and hawing, is to mutter
something about "taking a trip," or "taking a long nap," in hopes that
the child's curiosity will be satisfied. With regard to this typical parental
reaction, Edgar Jackson points out that the child is better able to cope
with the stress of limited, but accurate, knowledge of death than with the
misery and implied desertion resulting from the death of a love-object.[17]
Furthermore,

> Fears tend to be intensified when one cannot obtain direct, factual informa-
> tion and when questions are met by evasion or subterfuge.[18]

Regardless of the fact that the harm they may do is unintentional, most
American parents do not take an especially healthy approach to explaining death to their children. It has been suggested that most parents
either believe, or use as an excuse, the misconception that children have
no notion of death and that they therefore need no reassurance on the
subject. This belief and its implied behavior is strikingly similar to

> The certainty of a generation ago that the child had no sexual feelings and
> that, therefore, problems about childhood sexuality made no sense.[19]

Indeed, the comparison is frequently made between parents' reluctant,
evasive, and often confidence-destroying responses to their children's
questions about death and an earlier generation of parental responses
to questions concerning sex. Although one cannot deny that the situations
are analogous, one major difference makes talking about death the more
difficult task for parents: even if the parent had an equally strong desire
to talk about both topics in a straightforward manner, he has hopefully

had sexual experiences from which he can derive his answers, but does not have experience upon which to base an answer to the question, "What happens after I die?"

Thus, we find American parents unwilling and/or unable to talk to their children about death in a manner that will not produce anxiety. In fact, by evasion and deception, parents appear to be harming rather than helping their children in the development of their view of death. This fact becomes even clearer when it is realized that when children first come in contact with the death of animals, by themselves, and without the "help" of adults, the exposure is apparently non-problematical.[20]

If the American child obtains little or no parental direction and guidance in the formation of death attitudes, a question might be raised as to whether this is compensated for by the general culture. All available evidence points to the absence of clear cultural direction with respect to the "ultimate concern" in the United States. Bowman found that death and bereavement practices in this country, rather than being culturally routinized and transmitted, are to a great extent left to the individual.[21] In no known primitive culture is one so left to his own devices in facing his death; the primitive culture rather informs the individual as to what will happen to him when he dies.[22] Thus, with neither the parents nor the general culture offering instruction, the death attitude formation process of the American child is quite personalized.

Despite this marked individuation, attitudes become more sophisticated and fixed by the end of adolescence and during college age. They are still not unified into a close-knit pattern, however, since death continues to elicit strong and variable emotional responses. For example, when a group of adolescents were given a series of semantic differential tests, their responses to various concepts clustered or crystallized into meaningful wholes, with the exception of responses to 'death.' As Kastenbaum has shown, while other concepts are structured in a single framework, the concept of death lacks such organization.[23]

What may we therefore conclude concerning the formation of death attitudes in childhood? Given the existing state of knowledge on the topic, the most that we can reasonably infer is that individuals pass from a state of non-awareness to an increasingly clearer, though not necessarily unified, conception of death. Furthermore, underlying the development of death attitudes is a strong emotional involvement marked by fear, and, as parents and the general culture offer little direction, the specific content of the attitude formation process is left to the vagaries of the individual's experiences.

Unfortunately, we know even less about the direction and degree of attitude change in adult life. There is a pronounced paucity of research on these questions, probably because it is generally believed that as adults our attitudes are not as subject to marked changes as are those of children. However, we do know that there are at least two types of situations which can effectuate changes in an adult's attitude toward death.

The experience of "social death" is the first such situation. Loss of a close friend, relative, or loved one in adult life may be "experienced as the process of dying."[24] If we undergo this process of dying in a manner which is contrary to our existent attitudes, we may very well be compelled to change them. In addition, viewing a funeral may alter our attitudes toward our own deaths, for "rites performed for the dead generally have important effects for the living. A funeral ceremony is personal in its focus."[25]

Other situations which can cause attitudinal changes are those in which death threatens the individual himself. Death is thus brought closer to him and becomes more of a personal likelihood. This may happen in at least four different ways: The first such circumstance occurs when a person will apparently die in the next instant, as, for example, during a mine explosion, an earthquake, or an automobile accident. The second situation is one that "risks the fatal issue," such as combat, a surgical operation, a famine, or an armed robbery. The third and fourth are executions and terminal illnesses.[26] It should be pointed out that the knowledge of threatening death may not necessarily constitute a stress situation for some individuals; their death attitudes would therefore not change. As has been indicated elsewhere, the type of person the individual is and the death attitudes he holds may be more important than any degree of threat.[27] Furthermore, it should not be forgotten that the specific effects of a stress situation are dependent upon such variables as the kinds of coping techniques available to the individual, his emotional maturity, religious background, age, and socioeconomic status.[28] Finally, although there is as yet no definitive empirical support for this contention, it is logical to assume that the type and severity of threat, as well as the individual's perception of that threat, would constitute relevant explanatory variables. It would seem that the individual's perception of the threat is probably the most crucial of these variables: While a child holding a cap pistol and aiming it at one's face does not constitute a real threat, if one perceives the threat as real, the same effect on one's attitudes would result as would in the case of a real pistol.

While we have perhaps obtained an adequate comprehension of death attitude development and change for our present purposes, it is important to emphasize the lacunae of definitive knowledge and sound research on the topic. The need for further enlightened inquiry is especially pressing for

> Beliefs, attitudes and values are all organized together to form a functionally integrated cognitive system, so that a change in any part of the system will affect other parts, and will culminate in behavioral change.[29]

NOTES

1. H. Feifel, "The Taboo on Death," *American Behavioral Scientist,* 1963, 6, p. 67.
2. W. Bromberg and P. Schilder, "Death and Dying," *Psychoanalytic Review,* 1933, 20, p. 171.
3. J. C. Rheingold, *The Mother, Anxiety and Death.* Boston: Little, Brown and Company, Inc., 1967, p. 31.
4. I. E. Alexander and A. M. Alderstein, "Affective Responses to the Concept of Death in a Population of Children and Early Adolescents," *Journal of Genetic Psychology,* 1958, 93, pp. 168-169.
5. *Ibid.,* p. 176.
6. C. W. Wahl, "The Fear of Death," in Robert Fulton (ed.), *Death and Identity,* New York: John Wiley and Sons, Inc., 1965, p. 57. We would add here the observation that the nightly repetition of this prayer might well increase the child's fear, since it would remind him each night that he might die in his sleep.
7. H. Becker and D. K. Bruner, "Attitudes Toward Death and the Dead and Some Possible Causes of Ghost Fear," *Mental Hygiene,* 1931, 15, pp. 830-31.
8. Psychiatrists and psychologists have clearly indicated the relevance of one such traumatic event in the etiology of a now classic case of multiple personality, for example.
9. Alexander and Alderstein, *op. cit.,* pp. 168-169.
10. *Ibid.,* p. 169.
11. Refer, in this monograph, to Chapter Three for a thorough discussion of the fear of death, and Five for a treatment of methodological problems.
12. R. Cousinet, "L'Idée de la Mort chez les Enfants [The Idea of Death in Children]," *Journal of Normal and Pathological Psychology,* 1939, 36, pp. 65-75.
13. Alexander and Alderstein, *op. cit.,* p. 167.
14. M. H. Nagy, "The Child's View of Death," in Herman Feifel (ed.), *The Meaning of Death,* New York: McGraw-Hill Book Company, Inc., 1959, pp. 78-79.
15. Alexander and Alderstein, *op. cit.,* p. 169.
16. H. Feifel, "Death," *The Encyclopedia of Mental Health,* 1963, Vol. 2, p. 441.
17. E. N. Jackson, "Grief and Religion," in Herman Feifel (ed.), *The Meaning of Death, op. cit.,* pp. 218-233.
18. H. Feifel, "Death," *op. cit.,* p. 441.
19. *Ibid.,* p. 441.
20. Bromberg and Schilder, *op. cit.,* p. 174.
21. L. Bowman, *The American Funeral: A Study in Guilt, Extravagence, and Sublimity,* Washington, D. C.: Public Affairs Press, 1959.
22. J. W. Riley, Jr., "Death and Bereavement," *International Encyclopedia of the Social Sciences,* 1968, 4, p. 20.
23. R. Kastenbaum, "Time and Death in Adolescence," in Herman Feifel (ed.), *The Meaning of Death, op. cit.,* p. 103.
24. Rheingold, *op. cit.,* pp. 30-31.
25. D. G. Mandelbaum, "Social Uses of Funeral Rites," in Herman Feifel (ed.), *The Meaning of Death, op. cit.,* p. 189.

26. Rheingold, *op. cit.,* p. 35.
27. H. Feifel, "The Taboo on Death," *op. cit.,* pp. 66-67.
28. Rheingold, *op. cit.,* p. 36.
29. M. Rokeach, *Beliefs, Attitudes and Values,* San Francisco: Jossey-Bass, Inc., 1968, IX.

Chapter Two

The Fear of Death
and the Death Wish

*Perhaps there are persons who are immune
to the fear of death, but there are many more
who profess to be.*

Joseph C. Rheingold

The fear of death is one of the two major emotional responses to death,
the other being the death wish. Both of these reactions appear to under-
lie and direct death attitudes, although the precise manner in which they
do so remains, by and large, within the realm of conjecture. In fact, they
are so deeply and intricately intertwined with attitudes that many writers
refer to them as attitudes. As the way we feel emotionally about anything
predisposes us to certain beliefs and attitudes concerning it, we must first
appreciate the nature and significance of these two major emotional
undercurrents if we are to gain incisive and insightful knowledge of death
attitudes.

The fear of death

When writing about death, numerous authors have exhibited a tendency
to employ the terms 'fear of death' and 'death anxiety' interchangeably.
Not having found a satisfying explanation of this practice, we can only
conjecture that it results primarily from the manner in which death functions as a referent. In ordinary usage, a fear has a somewhat specific
referent. For example, one fears the approaching mugger, or one fears
spiders and rats. On the other hand, anxiety lacks a concrete referent;
one is not quite certain what is making him anxious. Death is sufficiently concrete for fear, sufficiently vague for anxiety. We fear the
specific referent, death, but death has many associations, such as dread
of the corpse, Hell, burial, loss of loved ones, and the pain of dying, all
of which are intermingled and generalized, creating an anxiety. For our
present purposes, therefore, 'fear of death' and 'death anxiety' will be
treated as synonymous, both referring to the intertwined phenomena. It
should be understood that when one is mentioned the other is also present.

17

There is, however, a distinction neglected by many writers and researchers that must be made in order that considerations might have validity.
Specifically, it is important to distinguish between the 'fear of death' and
the 'fear of dying.' It is possible, indeed highly probable, that some people
may fear the actual process of dying more than death itself, for dying may
be accompanied by pain, dependency on others, destruction of an attractive physical appearance, and shame.[1] When questioned as to how they
prefer to die, Americans typically respond, "quickly, with no suffering,
in one's bed, at home, sleeping at night."[2] Since there is demonstrable
concern as to the precise manner of death, there may also exist a certain
degree of fear about dying in ways contrary to our wishes. Although a
person's verbal denial of fear must be treated with appropriate skepticism,
due to the generally repressed nature of fear, one's admission of fear is
generally significant. Thus, statements such as, " 'I am afraid of dying
rather than of death or being dead,' " and " 'I have no fear whatever
about death, but dying is a different matter' " are instructive, for, while
we must employ extreme caution in the interpretation of verbal reports
concerning the fear of death, many of these clearly indicate the necessity
for distinguishing it from the fear of dying.[3]

Although we have pointed to the necessity for a clear distinction between the 'fear of death' and the 'fear of dying,' it is not our intention
to suggest that the latter in any way supersedes the former. Even though
the fear of dying, if not recognized, may operate to magnify the findings
of studies undertaken to determine the degree to which the fear of death
is manifested, the existence of the fear of dying makes the fear of death no
less real. Both factors may be present in the same individual, and the fear
of the process of dying may readily generalize to the fear of death itself.
Furthermore, the claim that he fears dying more than death may function
to disguise an individual's real fears simply because it is more socially
acceptable to admit to a fear of the former. For example, one group of
college students contended that they feared snakes and cancer more than
death, although in all probability these particular fears arise themselves
out of a fear of death.[4] People seem to fear

> ...not only the physically destructive aspects of death but also the expected
> loss of consciousness and self-control that it implies, as well as the loneliness
> and stamp of failure to which it dooms them. Others fear the forfeiture of their
> identity, their past and future, in addition to their present.[5]

To what extent can the fear of death be said to exist among men? Of
the scholars representing a variety of intellectual disciplines who have
been concerned with the question, a very substantial proportion consider
the fear of death to be virtually universal, or so prevalent as to be taken

as universal. A partial list of adherents includes Choron, Tillich, Seneca, Hartlan, Hocart, Malinowski, Capiro, Muller, Metschscikoff, Zilboorg, Chadwick, Capon, Alexander and Alderstein, and Greenberg and Klein. The universality of the fear of death is also well borne out in clinical work. In fact, so prevalent is the fear of death, that interested scholars, be they poets, scientists, or philosophers, have come increasingly to take its universality for granted.[6] We are thus compelled to concur with the observation made by Hattie Rosenthal, that

> ...many papers and studies could be cited, each touching on the fear of death, each a contribution which must lead us inevitably to the acknowledgement of the universality of this fear. This point has perhaps been sufficiently made.[7]

The fear of death has undeniable and important behavioral implications, since it constitutes an integral part of one's psychological make-up. Noted psychiatrist Gregory Zilboorg maintains that the fear of death is, "present in our mental functioning at all times." English psychoanalyst Melanie Klein felt that this fear lies at the root of human anxiety. Theologian Paul Tillich bases his theory of anxiety on the premise that man is finite and must die. Austrian psychiatrist William Steckel believes that in actuality every fear we have is the disguised fear of death.[8] So important is the fear of death to the psychology of the individual that some have insisted that it must enter into every psychoanalysis. Even when deeply repressed, the fear of death has many manifestations. Consequently,

> If thoughts and fears of death are left alone, they slide back, into the unconscious, and from there they operate as unseen enemies attacking from ambush.[9]

What explanation can be offered for the existence and prevalence of the death fear? Interestingly, many of the same reasons are given for the persistence of the death fear as have been suggested as original causes. A partial list of causative candidates includes such disparate phenomena as, "separation anxiety, sex guilt, physical restraint, fear of the dark, sibling rivalry, and the castration complex."[10] The acceptability of each of these potential explanations is problematical, however, for they tend to be nebulously derived and the relationship between them and the fear they ostensibly cause characteristically defies empirical interpretation.[11] Further doubt on their explanatory import is cast by the fact that many of these situations or traits are also frequently cited as effects or consequences of the death fear. For example, does one fear death as a consequence of a prior fear of the dark, or does the fear of the dark develop in response to the death fear?

Despite the logical and empirical problems of interpretation and verification, it is possible to isolate a small number of factors that do seem to play a particularly important role in adult maintenance of death fears. The first of these is the fear of the unknown. Death is perhaps the most mysterious and unknown of the unknowns, for unlike other situations, no one can report what happens after death; no one has ever died and lived to tell about it. There is some persuasive, although indirect, empirical support for the contention that it is the unknown component of death that is feared. It has been found, for example, that terminal patients who are told that they will soon die find it considerably easier to accept the certainty of death than the suspense of not knowing. It appears that in these cases, "...the unknown can be feared more than the most known, dreaded reality."[12] Further evidence in support of the causative role of the fear of the unknown is provided by reference to the study of a patient who was initially thought to be displaying a schizophrenic reaction of the catatonic variety: The patient often seemed to be in a stupor, immobile and silent. It was ultimately discovered, however, that what had appeared to be a catatonic stupor was really, "...a stratagem to provide her with 'rehearsals' of the death experience, in an attempt to alleviate her fear of death, the unknown."[13]

In addition to fearing the unknown, our fear of death seems to derive from our apprehension concerning the loss of those things we enjoy in life. We all have a variety of attachments to individuals and things in this world, connections which constitute much of what one considers his "self." It is therefore quite natural to fear the severence of these ties, which is inherent in death. This point becomes even more cogent when we consider how our attitudes toward death might be affected if we were assured that, "...the world would end for all when we die... that there is absolutely nothing that we would miss."[14]

Research evidence indicates that death is also feared because it signifies the end of opportunities to achieve goals and to finish projects which we hold dear, considerations which are quite important to one's self-esteem. In fact, it has been persuasively demonstrated that those who have attained most of their goals fear death the least.[15]

Another suggested component of the death fear is the dread of isolation or separation. As a *zoon politickon,* a human being has a fundamental need to relate to others of his kind. To the individual, death represents the ultimate separation, an isolation total and perpetual. Man therefore fears the aloneness of death.[16] In this regard, it has also been found that when the separation fears of children are aroused, their fear of death increases significantly.[17] There is good reason to believe that this fear of separation may be an especially strong component of the American fear of death. Numerous students of American culture have commented upon the growing tendency toward "belonging" and "other directedness." So strong and pervasive is the American desire to participate in groups that the dominant fear in the nation seems to have undergone a radical transformation from the fear of castration to the fear of ostracism. Dr. May reports that a large number of his patients, particularly those from Madison avenue, choose

> ...to be castrated, that is, to give up his [their] power, in order not to be ostracized. The real threat is not to be accepted, to be thrown out of the group, to be left solitary and alone.[18]

At least three other reasons for the maintenance of adult death fears have been suggested: the fear of losing consciousness (loss of self-mastery), fear of punishment (Hell), and fear of what will become of one's dependents.[19] It would seem, therefore, that the fear of death is most appropriately understood as having a multidimensional, rather than a unidimensional, determination.[20] Regardless of the etiological uncertainties, however, the result is a very strong and deep-rooted fear from which no man is exempt.

While great in all men, the strength of the death fear is nonetheless subject to some degree of variation. Although differences in the degree to which we fear death are due largely to our individual experiences with it, some relevant variables have been isolated. For example, people seem to fear death most between the ages of forty and sixty. During that period there is much to be accomplished and much to live for, yet death is viewed as rapidly approaching. Adolescents appear to fear death the least because they are too busy to spend much time thinking about it, and because they can be reasonably sure of a full life ahead. To the adolescent, therefore, death is conceived as too remote to be perceived as an immediate threat.[21]

In addition to age, a second source of variation may be found in the nature and degree of social support one has in facing his own death. It has been discovered that elderly people living with a relative in familiar surroundings, or even in homes for the aged, are less apprehensive about their deaths than are those who live alone.[22] This observation is especially interesting from the perspective of American society, where there has been an increasing tendency to segregate the elderly and to hospitalize or isolate the dying.

Another study of the aged found that those who stated that they feared death, as opposed to those who did not admit to such a fear, had: fewer leisure activities, feelings of rejection and depression, lower full-scale I.Q., lower performance I.Q., fewer normal Rorschach responses, less belief in an afterlife, and read the Bible less frequently.[23] These findings warrant cautious interpretation, however, for it is important to bear in mind that these factors are associated with the subjects' articulated admission of the fear of death. Since this fear is ordinarily highly repressed, it is not unreasonable to suppose that the aforementioned factors may account for the willingness to admit to the death fear rather than for its strength.

Certain groups have been found to fear death more than others. Soldiers reveal a significantly more marked fear than members of other occupations, probably because they are exposed to death and are personally threatened by it frequently. One study of combat personnel during the Korean War uncovered an interesting variety of individual defenses against the fear of death, including the adoption of a fatalistic attitude or of the myth that one is invulnerable, the use of superstition, a reliance on religious belief and faith, and apathy.[24]

Anomalously, a second group which appears to fear death more than others is physicians. When compared to control groups of patients and normal subjects, for example, physicians were found to think about death less, yet fear it more, than either control group. On the one hand, they probably think about death less as a counterphobic defense to relieve the emotional strain of the tragedy they see so frequently. On the other hand, it has been hypothesized that individuals enter the medical profession because they fear death more than others and hope to acquire the knowledge to protect themselves from death.[25] Alternatively, of course, it may be argued that the physician's greater death fear might result, like his counterphobic defense, from his regular exposure to death.

Religion constitutes yet another variable which has been found to correlate with the intensity of the death fear. A substantial number of studies have been conducted indicating, variously, that religion either increases or decreases the fear of death.[26] Riley has suggested that these investigations are inconclusive and contradictory for a variety of reasons: Various specialized populations have been studied, different definitions of death are emphasized by different religions, and differing needs are met by religion in divers parts of the country.[27] One might add to Riley's list the observations that definitions of death within religions are currently shifting, that the strength of socialization differs among the various religions as well as individually, and that the specific research techniques employed have varied, thereby increasing the likelihood of eliciting dissimilar responses. Compounding these problems are two factors which make suspect or dubious the findings of those studies undertaken to investigate the effect of religion on death fears: First, those researchers who have been involved with the question have characteristically ignored the fact that they may very well be dealing with a "chicken-egg" controversy. For example, suppose in a concrete research situation one discovers a high positive correlation between the fear of death and religiosity, that is, the most religious are found to exhibit the strongest death fears. How is such a finding to be interpreted? Does the evidence necessarily force the conclusion that religiosity increases the fear of death, or is it more appropriate to argue that those who are most religious are so because of a stronger death fear? A second factor which operates to obfuscate the entire question is a technical problem of some import. Specifically, these studies have prompted and provided for responses which have been interpreted as indicating either increased fear, or decreased fear, and occasionally neither. Seldom, if ever, has the possibility been entertained that religion may *both* increase *and* decrease fear simultaneously. This consideration becomes particularly cogent when it is realized that most religions in the United States provide a "heaven" which might reduce fears and a "hell" which might very well increase them. Robert Fulton probably had something similar in mind when advancing the claim that religion, "...plays a dual role in a person's attitudes toward death. Religion for the deeply devout person may be 'functional' and supportive, or it may be 'dysfunctional'..."[28] Furthermore, even though an individual may be quite firmly convinced that his proper place in an afterlife would be heaven, his fear of death would be likely to persist, varying with the degree of certainty of his belief in a afterlife.

Despite the problematical nature of the religious variable, others such as age, social support, and membership in various occupational groups do indeed seem to affect the degree to which individuals fear death. In any event, as was suggested by our earlier mention of the defense mechanisms of combat troops, the death fear manifests itself in many ways. Interestingly, a causal nexus has been hypothesized and purportedly demonstrated between the fear of death and asthma.[29] Furthermore, it has been claimed that the fear of death assumes such varied forms as fear of separation, mutilation, and abandonment; neurotic and somatic complaints; depressed moods; overconsideration for one's family; fear of loss in general, of leaving one's house and of flying in a plane; and schizophrenic denial of reality, to cite but a few.[30] The specific manifestations of death fears appear nearly as varied as the individuals who possess them. Thus, the fear of death is "...a very complex thing with conscious, preconscious and unconscious aspects and all sorts of predetermining cultural, historical and religious factors."[31]

There are certain fears that are so universal, or so nearly so, that a society comes to consider them as natural or rational. Ostensibly, the fear of death is one of these in American society.[32] Death, in both its process and product, is not a very attractive proposition, and it is natural that we fear it. Marcuse indicates that this emotion is quite rational,

> ...in view of the fact that death is not only inevitable but also incalculable, ubiquitous, and the tabooed limit of human freedom. All anxiety is fear, fear of a real, omnipresent danger, the most rational attitude and feeling.[33]

Of course, this view of the normality of the death fear is consistent with the research results supporting its universality. It is instructive to note that the degree of mental disturbance in tested patients does not appear to affect the intensity of their death fears, for the fear of death seems to be present in equal degrees in mentally disturbed persons and in normal subjects.[34] In a similar vein, the degree of mental illness apparently has no effect on overall death attitudes.[35]

Not only does the available evidence overwhelmingly support the contention that Americans interpret death fears as natural, but a strong and convincing argument can be made for the claim that it is extremely advantageous from a societal point of view that this be the case. In fact, the fear of death is important for the maintenance of society and is a necessary ingredient for social cohesion, since "No domination is complete without the threat of death and the recognized right to dispense death–death by legal verdict, in war, by starvation."[36] The threat of death is obviously meaningless if the members of a society do not fear it, and many laws have little or no meaning unless both the threat and the fear are present. Furthermore, it has even been argued that it is beneficial for a society to recognize and condone the death fear because of the contributions which it purportedly makes to societal progress.[37] For example, because man fears death he builds shelter for protection from storms, finds cures for diseases, avoids accidents by instituting traffic laws, and the like. In short, the American view of the death fear as natural or rational is apparently both accurate and valuable.

Although it may readily be conceded that the fear of death is rational, it must also be recognized that it is also quite capable of causing problems for the individual, problems which may result in a wide variety of mild to severe personality disorders. Unfortunately, knowing that the fear is rational does not alter the fact of its continued existence; while recognition of its normalcy may make the fear easier to bear, it does not function to overcome it. In fact, the mere acknowledgement of its necessity and rationality may very well preclude its dissipation, since it might come to be viewed as insurmountable.

The death wish

The antithesis of the fear of death is the death wish, the second major emotional response to death. Throughout history, in myths, ballads, novels, and other forms of human expression, characters have often been portrayed as wishing to die, with death frequently being conceived as a compelling and exciting adventure or a thing of great beauty. Like these figures, Charles Wesley saw excellence in death, as the following portion of one of his poems reveals:

> Ah! lovely Appearance of Death!
> No Sight upon Earth is so fair.
> Not all the gay Pageants that breathe
> Can with a dead Body compare.[38]

It should be emphasized that the death wish is distinct and distinguishable from the desire to commit suicide. While the yearning in each case may be equally earnest and the ultimate goal of both is death, they are distinct in that they stem from dissimilar motivations. Specifically, whereas the motivation behind the death wish is considered normal, the desire to commit suicide ordinarily stems from abnormal impulses–to get even with a loved one or to gain attention. Too, the death wish is somewhat more passive in nature than the desire to commit suicide; while one may wish to die he will not actually kill himself, whereas the desire to suicide leads to positive and purposive action.

Freud was probably the first social scientist of note to seriously and systematically consider the death wish. He hypothesized that man contains within himself an innate desire to die, "the death instinct." Within the psyche, this death instinct, *thanatos,* was said to exist in direct opposition to the desire to preserve life, *eros.* Freud considered the death instinct to be quite as universal as the fear of death.[39] This conceptualization has generally been rejected by contemporary social scientists: A survey of psychological abstracts dating from 1931 to 1961 revealed that the concept of 'the death instinct' had been rejected by a margin of three to one.[40] Even Freud's successors and staunchest supporters have by and large discarded the notion.[41] Although the reasons for this repudiation are many, perhaps the most significant relate to the role which 'the death instinct' plays in Freud's psychoanalytic theory, where it "...operates silently within the organism and becomes fused with the life instinct, or expresses itself as aggression."[42] Indeed, the existence and precise effects of a hidden, fused, and nonobservable death instinct are difficult to substantiate empirically. Moreover, the typical social scientific position concerning instinctive behavior has undergone a radical transformation since the time of Freud, for much of what was previously thought to be due to instinct has been found to originate in universal experience.

Although it is necessary to concede the problematical nature of Freud's early conceptualization, such an acknowledgement does not alter the fact that the wish to die is still very real in men. As Rheingold has clearly indicated, despite the fact that "...the impulsion toward death is experiential in origin, it is deep rooted and as nearly universal as the fear of death... [and] wish and fear constitute an ambivalence."[43] While no recent investigations into the prevalence of the death wish are available for consideration, it is likely that the findings of a 1933 study continue to be applicable to contemporary American society, at least in broad outline. Bromberg and Schilder found that, almost universally, individuals have consciously wished to die at some point in their lives, most commonly in response to frustration. The failure of a few respondents to admit to ever having had such a wish was interpreted by Bromberg and Schilder as probably resulting from suppression.[44]

The death wish manifests itself multifariously in everyday life. It is reflected in many of our unconscious choices, in certain modes of adjustment, in some types of anti-social behavior, in accident-proneness, in addictions, in many reactions to stress, in neurosis and depressive states, and in certain psychosomatic disorders.[45] Indeed, the existence of a highly prevalent and virtually universal death wish seems no longer in doubt, as most interested students are now occupied with culling out and investigating those factors which affect the degree to which individuals wish for death.

Of the several hypotheses which have been ventured to explain variations in the intensity of the death wish, only two seem to possess sufficient validity to warrant serious consideration. First, the intensity of the death wish appears to be positively related to the "pro-secular" and negatively related to the "pro-sacred." In other words, the fewer and less salient one's sacred values and beliefs, the stronger and more overt his wish for death. Conversely, greater involvement with and commitment to the realm of the sacred favor a weaker death wish.[46] This relationship probably obtains in part because pro-sacred values and beliefs may include notions of judgment and hell, which are undesirable. Furthermore, in the United States, there exist salient, sacred values which include prohibitions against the wish to die. For example, it is felt that one must fulfill certain obligations on Earth before he may be rewarded in an afterlife, and it is regularly believed that God should be the only judge of when one will die. One should be cautious not to interpret these remarks as inferring that individuals whose values are oriented toward the pro-sacred do not also maintain a death wish, for the difference is but one of degree. In this regard, it is well to bear in mind that, compared with a trying life, heaven may well be appealing and, "...even negative connotations of death, as in the expectation of eternal punishment in hell fire, serve to gratify urges to punish oneself for misbehavior."[47]

Sex constitutes the second important factor related to the degree or intensity of the death wish. Females have characteristically exhibited a stronger death wish than have males. Women are more likely to look forward to death "with a sense of excitement;" death simultaneously frightens and thrills them to roughly equal degrees.[48] In describing how her thinking about death changed during her lifetime, Sarah Cleghorn provides insights into the female death wish. During her thirties Miss

Cleghorn began thinking about death as "a pleasurable adventure." Since her life had always been good and was constantly improving, it seemed natural to her that her death would be "a still more abounding experience." She recalls going to tea with a much older woman and envying her because she would probably "enjoy before the rest of us the prime adventure of dying." She also tells of an old woman whom she knew who had outlived all her friends and was quite disappointed about being left alive and alone. Ostensibly, the old woman's emotions registered hurt anger, "like a schoolgirl left out of a picnic." In the conclusion of her article, Miss Cleghorn claims that her feelings toward death had changed, yet her death wish seemed to be still with her. Her final sentence states that death should "prove the moment of keenest pleasure that we have ever known."[49]

There is substantial empirical support for the hypothesis that women, like Miss Cleghorn, wish for death more than men do. For example, one study revealed that death has sexual connotations for women, thereby providing a partial explanation of why their desire for it exceeds that of men. To women, death is apparently both attractive and repulsive, for it is viewed as a "lustry, but evil, seducer of women."[50] Yet another study compared a group of critically ill female patients with female patients having minor ailments who were soon to be discharged. It was found that

> The women for whom death was a real possibility *thought almost twice as often* about punishment and illicit sex as the women who were about to go home after minor illness.[51]

Further support for the argument is provided by the results of a pilot study which showed that college women considered the metaphorical view of death as a "gay seducer" far more accurate than those chosen by college men—"grinning butcher," or "understanding doctor."[52]

That women are more likely to view death as a lover is apparently due to the manner in which we personify death. Pound's discussion indicates that the American culture contains seven major personifications of death, such as the reaper or the devil, not one of them being a female.[53] This lack of a female personification of death probably precludes males from attaching sexual significance to death, thereby leading to sex differentials with respect to the death wish.

Although apparently somewhat stronger in women, the death wish is, as indicated earlier, practically universal, and the accumulated evidence to date sheds really very little light on those factors responsible for variations in its intensity. It is perhaps appropriate to note here that the argument has been advanced that the death wish often results, not from some unique or independent desire for death, but rather from the dislike of life. In other words, we look to death because we feel that life has failed us.[54]

Regardless of its specific origin or origins, however, the fact remains that man frequently wishes death, consciously or unconsciously. We are therefore caught up in a fundamental and exceedingly significant emotional contradiction. While on the one hand we often wish for death, on the other hand we fear it. Somehow, we must all cope with this ambivalent emotional state, and it is fruitful to view our attitudes toward death as one means toward this end. For example,

> There are various ways of attempting to cope with the fear of death. We may try to ignore it; we never mention it, and always attempt to turn our thoughts in another direction when we find ourselves dwelling on it... Or we may adopt the exactly opposite course and meditate continually on the brevity of human life, in the hope that familiarity will breed contempt.[55]

In the remaining chapters, we will seek to determine how Americans cope with their emotional responses to death in terms of their attitudes. Specifically, we will be concerned with the acceptance-denial question.

NOTES

1. H. Feifel, "Death," *The Encyclopedia of Mental Health,* 1963, Vol. 2, p. 438.
2. *Ibid.,* p. 433.
3. The two statements cited are reported in W. Bromberg and P. Schilder, "Death and Dying," *Psychoanalytic Review,* 1933, 20, p. 148.
4. M. H. Means, "Fears of One Thousand College Women," *Journal of Abnormal and Social Psychology,* 1936, 31, pp. 291-311.
5. Feifel, *op. cit.,* p. 438.
6. J. C. Rheingold, *The Mother, Anxiety and Death,* Boston: Little, Brown and Company, Inc., 1967, pp. 48-50.
7. H. Rosenthal, "The Fear of Death as an Indispensable Factor in Psychotherapy," *American Journal of Psychotherapy,* 1963, 17, p. 621.
8. These observations are from Feifel, *op. cit.,* p. 438.
9. Rosenthal, *op. cit.,* p. 621.
10. J. W. Riley, Jr., "Death and Bereavement," *International Encyclopedia of the Social Sciences,* 1968, Vol. 4, p. 23.
11. See Chapter Five for a more detailed discussion of methodological problems.
12. H. Feifel, "The Taboo on Death," *American Behavioral Scientist,* 1963, 6, p. 67.
13. Rosenthal, *op. cit.,* p. 624
14. W. Kaufmann, "Existentialism and Death," in Herman Feifel (ed.), *The Meaning of Death,* New York: McGraw-Hill Book Company, Inc., 1959, p. 62.
15. J. C. Diggory and D. Z. Rothman, "Values Destroyed by Death," *Journal of Abnormal and Social Psychology,* 1961, 63, p. 209.

16. Rosenthal, *op. cit.,* p. 625.
17. R. P. Ross, "Separation Fear and the Fear of Death in Children," *Dissertation Abstracts,* 1966, XXVII, pp. 2878b-2879b.
18. R. May, *Psychology and the Human Dilemma,* Princeton, N. J.: D. Van Nostrand Co., Inc., 1967, p. 120.
19. G. Murphy, "Discussion," in Herman Feifel (ed.), *The Meaning of Death, op. cit.,* pp. 334-335.
20. Rheingold, *op. cit.,* p. 62.
21. H. Feifel, "Death," *op. cit.,* p. 431. Actually, adolescent fear of death may be very prevalent but quite repressed, since it is seldom brought to the conscious level at this age.
22. Riley, *op. cit.,* p. 23.
23. F. C. Jeffers, C. R. Nichols and C. Eisdorfer, "Attitudes of Older Persons Toward Death: A Preliminary Study," *Journal of Gerontology,* 1961, 16, pp. 53-56.
24. H. Feifel, "Death," *op. cit.,* p. 445. A friend in Viet Nam adds to this list a common reaction which he has seen–getting angry at death and the war as a defense against fear.
25. *Ibid.,* p. 445.
26. Riley, *op. cit.,* p. 23.
27. *Ibid.,* p. 23.
28. R. L. Fulton, "Introduction: Attitudes and Responses toward Death," in Robert Fulton (ed.), *Death and Identity,* New York: John Wiley and Sons, Inc., 1965, p. 81.
29. K. J. Monsour, "Asthma and the Fear of Death," *Psychoanalytic Quarterly,* 1960, 29, pp. 56-71.
30. H. Feifel, "Death," *op. cit.,* p. 439.
31. Murphy, *op. cit.,* p. 335.
32. A. D. Weisman and T. P. Hackett, "Predilection to Death," in Fulton, *op. cit.,* p. 317. While we consider the fear of death natural, we do not expect it to be admitted readily, since this fear is characteristically perceived as indicative of personal weakness. In this society, virtue consists of the absence of weakness, in large part.
33. H. Marcuse, "The Ideology of Death," in Herman Feifel (ed.), *The Meaning of Death, op. cit.,* p. 71.
34. H. Feifel, "Death," *op. cit.,* p. 439.
35. H. Feifel, "Attitudes of Mentally Ill Patients Toward Death," in Fulton, *op. cit.,* p. 141.
36. Marcuse, *op. cit.,* p. 73.
37. *Ibid.,* p. 71.
38. Cited in C. Driver, "The Great Unmentionable," *Atlas,* August, 1965, 10, p. 113.
39. R. Fulton and G. Geis, "Death and Social Values," in Fulton, *op. cit.,* p. 69.
40. M. Williams, "Changing Attitudes toward Death: A Survey of Contributions in Psychological Abstracts Over a Thirty Year Period," *Journal of Human Relations,* 1966, 19, p. 409.
41. Fulton and Geis, *op. cit.,* p. 70.

42. Rheingold, *op. cit.,* p. 57.
43. *Ibid.,* p. 58.
44. Bromberg and Schilder, *op. cit.,* p. 149.
45. Rheingold, *op. cit.,* p. 58.
46. R. A. Kalish, "An Approach to the Study of Death Attitudes," *American Behavioral Scientist,* 1963, 6, p. 69.
47. D. C. McClelland, "The Harlequin Complex," in Robert White (ed.), *The Study of Lives,* New York: Atherton Press, 1963, p. 96.
48. *Ibid.,* p. 95.
49. See S. Cleghorn, "Changing Thoughts of Death," *Atlantic Monthly,* 1923, 132, pp. 810-812.
50. McClelland, *op. cit.,* p. 107.
51. E. S. Greenberger, "Fantasies of Women Confronting Death: A Study of Critically Ill Patients," Unpublished Doctoral Dissertation, Radcliffe College, 1961, summarized in White, *op. cit.,* pp. 107-113.
52. *Ibid.*
53. L. Pound, "American Euphemisms for Dying, Death and Burial: An Anthology," *American Speech,* 1936, 11, p. 197.
54. H. Feifel, "Death," *op. cit.,* p. 446.
55. B. Russell, "Your Child and the Fear of Death," *The Forum,* 1929, 81, p. 174.

PART TWO

THE
ACCEPTANCE-DENIAL
CONTROVERSY

Chapter Three

The American Denial of Death

One cannot look directly at either the sun or death.

de la Rochefoucauld

To the man in the street, at least in twentieth-century America, it [death] is something to avoid thinking about so far as possible, to push under the rug, to deny with phrases like 'passed on' or with elaborate rituals symbolic of immortality.

David McClelland

Many persons engaged in death research suggest, either explicitly or implicitly, that Americans cope with their emotional responses to death by developing an attitude of denial of their own deaths. By adopting the attitude that death will not come to them, they can live their lives free of the fear of death, at least on the conscious level. Theologian Paul Tillich argues that this is the attitude that most of us hold, and that Americans react to the fearful and inescapable end of their lives by looking only into the immediate future,

...while cutting off from our awareness the future which is farther away, and above all, by cutting off from our consciousness the end, the last moment of our future.[1]

Tillich is not alone in his opinion that the characteristic American attitude toward death is one of denial. Many writers suggest that the individual does not, as a rule, view death as a reality to be accepted, but rather as a fantasy, something that will happen to others but not to himself. Through painstaking research as well as evaluation of more casual evidence derived from observations of everyday American life, they arrive at conclusions similar to the following reached by Wahl:

We flee from the reality of our eventual death with such purpose and persistence and we employ defenses so patently magical and regressive that these would be ludicrously obvious... in any other area of human conflict.[2]

Supporters of the death denial contention tend to feel that most Americans hold attitudes which are very similar to those given by respondents in an early study conducted by Bromberg and Schilder. A few representative responses should suffice to provide the reader with an adequate grasp of what is considered indicative of a typical death denial attitude:

> "It [the respondent's own death] is the remotest fantasy. How can people exist when I'm not here? I can't die."
>
> "I most emphatically suppress the thought of my own death."
>
> "At times it seems unreal and I am protected in the thought that I am to have a long life."
>
> "No, my death is not probable. I feel, if I keep thinking 'I am still living,' that I'll never die." [3]

The basic attitude conveyed by the subjects quoted above is that they will live forever. Death for them appears unreal and mythical; they deny its existence as it applies to themselves. Some students of death research claim that not only do Americans deny the reality of their own deaths, but also that American culture supports this denial. It is not a matter of pure coincidence that Americans share this attitude, it is argued, for the tendency of our culture, in the presence of death, has been

> ...to run, hide, and seek refuge in group norms and actuarial statistics. The individual face of death has become blurred by embarrassed curiosity and institutionalization. [4]

What evidence has been and can be mustered in support of the argument that both Americans and their culture deny the reality of death? Before we proceed with a systematic discussion of this considerable evidence, it should be pointed out that although our primary concern is with the attitudes of Americans toward their own deaths, we will frequently refer to their attitudes toward death in the generic sense. Although these attitudinal domains should be kept analytically distinct, it should also be recognized that it is likely that they are very much intertwined empirically: It is highly probable that our attitudes toward our own deaths tend to generalize to death in general. Reciprocally, our attitudes toward our own deaths are, to a large extent, supported by the cultural view of death in general.

Evidence in support of the death denial argument

American denial of death apparently manifests itself quite early in life, during childhood as well as in adolescence. Many of the games which

American children play seem to deal with death. Whereas one might casually interpret this phenomenon as testimony to the fact that children in America tend to accept the existence of death, it should be noted that the death theme in games is not real to the participants. Death itself is a sort of game that one can stop playing at will, thus denying its reality. Because children do not view death as a permanent or infinite state, they experience no evident difficulty in their recurrent decisions to "banish" death. This banishment is most apparent in games such as "cowboys and Indians," where the child at one moment has been shot dead, and in the next moment comes back to life.[5] In addition to exemplifying actual death denial, such games may also serve as teaching devices whereby the child learns to deny death.

The theme of violent death and its magical reversability runs like a leitmotif through much of our children's fairy tales and folk literature.[6] Often the dead hero comes back to life, thanks to some magical potion or spell, or because a good fairy or spirit felt that the hero's life was valuable. Thus, the literature of the American Culture provides the child with a concept of death as an illusion, as something that can be undone. In addition to telling us something of the child's needs and attitudes, however, this literature also provides suggestive information about American adults, for it is they who are its authors. In a similar vein, one need only turn on the endless cartoons on television Saturday morning to witness further reinforcement of death denial produced by adults and consumed by children. Heroes and villains alike are shot with rifles, crushed by gigantic boulders, blown to pieces by dynamite, bombarded with cannon balls, and pushed off cliffs, only to jump to their feet (after the *laughter* stops) to be "killed" again.

Adolescents also deny their own deaths, a denial probably due, at least in part, to their conception of time. An extremely intense present seems to obscure the adolescent's future so that " 'now' is so real a problem that both past and future are pallid by comparison."[7] With even the immediate future so hard to grasp, the death of the adolescent in the distant future is virtually incomprehensible and certainly not a reality with which to be concerned.

This denial of death continues to exist throughout the lives of Americans; moreover, the culture is imbued with numerous expressions of this denial. One of the more striking examples of this cultural denial is the taboo on conversation concerning death, noted as early as 1936 by Pound. A lover of language, Pound could not resist slipping some puns into his discussion of euphemisms; yet his analysis was filled with excellent insights, many of which hold true to this day. He states,

It appears, in fact, that one of mankind's gravest problems is to avoid straightforward mention of dying or burial. Every ingenuity is practiced to find words which will shroud the idea of death.[8]

Jessica Mitford's controversial treatment of *The American Way of Death* provides countless examples of how the funeral industry, and the American people, still refer to death euphemistically.[9] Funeral directors call themselves "grief therapists," the room where the body is laid out "the slumber room," and the total scene of the casket, flowers, and corpse, "a loving memory picture." The euphemistic manner in which we handle death exemplifies the proscription against talking directly about death; it reveals our desire to protect ourselves from the reality that is death. In most modern secular societies, including ours, death is not considered to be an "open or polite topic of conversation, except among the aged..."[10] Immediately following the death of an individual, it is apparently taboo for those around the deceased, even the elderly, to talk about death. It is startling to note that in interviews with acute geriatric patients, as many as 87% stated that they had *never* talked about death or dying before.[11]

The taboo on death conversation may be due in part to the somewhat superstitious feeling or belief that if we do not talk about something, it does not exist. Our behavior seems to support this view, for, as one writter contends, "In all our actions we evince the belief that as long as we keep quiet about it, death itself will 'pass away.'"[12] Regardless of the fact that avoidance of death as a topic of conversation does not in reality render it nonexistent, this lack of discussion does have a tendency to remove death from our conscious thoughts. By succeeding in our attempts to avoid thoughts of death, we do in fact deny death the status of an eventuality which will have to be faced. This taboo on death conversation has carried over in some measure into a taboo on concern about death as well, and, as a result, "we have been compelled, in an unhealthy measure, to internalize our thoughts and feelings, fears, and even hopes concerning death."[13]

Thus it can be seen that the American taboo on death conversation reflects our denial of the reality of death; indeed it is a product of this denial. If it is reasonable to so view this taboo as a product of the American death denial, it seems also reasonable to assume that it, along with many other manifestations of death denial, may reciprocally be viewed as a causative or contributory factor in the existence or persistence of death denial. A somewhat complementary process may be at work here: While on the one hand we proscribe death conversation because we deny the existence of death, on the other hand we are reinforced in our denial, since the taboo on talking about death ensures that we are seldom forced to admit its existence. Therefore, the taboo on death conversation in America may contribute to death denial as well as reflect it.

Denial of death is further revealed by the manner in which our society customarily deals with death and the dying. Americans tend to segregate death, removing it, like a kind of "noxious disease," from their immediate experience. The aged of our society, the most susceptible to death, are frequently relegated to homes for the aged and retirement villages, where they are left "to await fate in the same manner as the leper once did."[14]

Hospital practices also serve as useful indices of our society's denial of death. For example, numerous techniques have been developed to hide the fact of death in high mortality wards. Bodies are never removed during visiting hours, to ensure that visitors will not have to view death. Patients are similarly protected from death contacts, as ward-mates nearing death are removed to private rooms. Sometimes death comes unexpectedly and is noticed by those sharing the victim's room before it is discovered by the staff; such incidents are "considered troublesome since elaborate techniques are required to remove the corpse without offending the living."[15] The intended result of such techniques is to make death invisible and to thus render it nonexistent.

In a textbook on *Modern Concepts in Hospital Administration,* a section describing the proper location for the morgue is highly suggestive of death denial in American hospitals:

> The hospital morgue is best located on the ground floor and placed in an area inaccessible to the general public. It is important that the unit have a suitable exit leading onto a private loading platform which is concealed from the hospital **patient** and the general public.[16]

Once again the hospital evidently assumes that death should not be viewed by the public. Although one might argue that such practices might be due in part to a public relations effort aimed at bolstering the hospital's image of efficiency and effectiveness (by hiding its "mistakes"), certainly if the American public accepted death there would be no need for such carefully planned concealment.

Death is made still more invisible and seemingly nonexistent by the hospital's doctors. When we observe a physician administering drugs to a patient, we quite naturally assume that he does so because the drugs will either ease the patient's pain or aid in his treatment. This, however, is not always the case, for even when drugs are necessary neither for the patient's treatment nor to reduce his pain, "drugs are sometimes administered to reduce the disruptiveness of his passing..."[17]

The actions of nurses function both to conceal death from others and to reflect their own denial of death. Richard Kalish has provided some indications of their characteristic behavior: one geriatric nurse he studied "*never* upsets a patient by telling him of the death of a close friend or ward-mate |thus leaving him to contemplate the significance of the empty bed|."[18] Another nurse, this time a male, relieved himself of having to think about a patient who was going to die by unloading the knowledge on the patient herself. He told the woman abruptly and without feeling, as was his practice, that she was to die in three months of cancer (it took six). In a final example, a nursing home aide is reputed to have removed thoughts of death by taking "a stiff shot" after work to "forget about that depressing place."[19] Kalish's most ingenious test lends support to the contention that to maintain death denial, one must avoid contact with death as much as possible, lest the reality of death become too obvious. In order to determine the extent to which nurses avoid the dying, he compared the length of time it took nurses to respond to the call lights of terminal patients as opposed to non-terminal patients. Kalish reports that, "...the nurses, although not the observer, were startled to learn how much they delayed answering the ring of the dying."[20]

The manner in which our society cares for its dying does indeed seem to reflect the kind of attitude that supporters of the death denial argument claim is prevalent throughout the United States. Our treatment of the elderly and the hospital's routinized care of the dead and dying, coupled with the attitudes and behaviors of the doctors and nurses who administer to the dying, reveal tendencies or desires to isolate, segregate, hide and ignore death. A society which accepts death would be unlikely to behave in this fashion.

A critical examination of the individual and cultural reactions to the dead shows that American funeral customs and the related funeral industries also mask the reality of death. Much of this evidence is again highly suggestive and supportive of the death denial contention.

Persons who accept the reality of death, and therefore a cessation of the physical self, should have no concern for physical protection and comfort after death. Our use of caskets, however, is a manifestation of the attitude that death does not really put an end to physical experience. The type of casket which Americans most often buy is one of the impermeable variety offered by the funeral industry, "' solid copper–a quality casket which offers superb value to the client seeking long-lasting protection.'"[21] Evidently, when Americans say they will die, they really feel that they will take a long nap. As a result of this belief, casket manufacturers like Elgin can profit heavily from their "revolutionary 'Perfect posture' bed" or can find great success selling the "Colonial Classic beauty–18 guage lead-coated steel... Some are equipped with foam rubber, some with inner spring mattresses."[22] The American apparently does not die, he simply sleeps very soundly.

In the same way that our choice of caskets may be viewed as symptomatic of death denial, our customary way of handling funerals may also be taken as a reflection of this denial. Rather than having direct contact with the dead, Americans normally engage others to take care of the disposal ritual, and,

> By assigning professional functionaries the responsibility for traditional familial roles, contemporary society not only avoids direct and disconcerting contact with death itself, but also, more important, permits its members to avoid close and disturbing confrontation with the inconsistencies inherent in their traditional theological explanations and emerging secular viewpoints.[23]

By thus paying others to take care of our dead, we are enabled not only to deny death, but also to evade many of the problems which arise from thinking about death. In addition to being indicative of death denial, however, this shift in the responsibility for treatment of the dead from the family to trained professionals is also a function of the general changes within the industrial society's family system, in which many traditional family functions are being transferred to other institutions.

Other varied funeral practices also reflect American death denial. The use of euphemisms for death, discussed earlier in this chapter, occurs with near-predictable regularity throughout the funeral period. When the funeral party reaches the cemetery they do not ordinarily view the casket itself, which would remind them that death has come to the individual within it, for the casket is hidden by flowers. Formerly in the United States the reality of death was reinforced by the lowering of the casket into the grave; this practice functioned to remind onlookers that the person being buried would be covered with earth, never to return to life. Currently, however, it is general practice not to lower the casket until all those connected with the "deceased" person have left the cemetery.

A final illustration of how American funeral practices lend themselves to death denial is seen in the funeral industry's willing compliance with the public's desire to make the corpse appear to be quite alive, rather than to show it just as it really is. In the past, certain types of clothes were worn by the corpse, a signal to the viewers that the corpse was indeed dead; these symbolic clothes made the denial of death quite difficult. Traditional death clothing is no longer used: The contemporary corpse is garbed in attire made to give the impression of life. Shrouds have been replaced by hand-made original fashions ranging from stylish suits for men to negligees and cocktail dresses for the ladies. The characteristic death pallor of the corpse, which formerly indicated the presence of death to the onlooker, is now covered up by a wide variety of grooming techniques and products such as "Nature-Glo—the ultimate in cosmetic embalming."[24]

Despite the apparent support given the death denial argument by these funeral customs, one should refrain from making the assumption that the denial of death is the sole causative or contributory factor as regards such practices as cosmetic embalming. These customs might also be a result of the desire on the part of family and friends to give the viewers a good impression of the "deceased". First impressions may be important, but so are last impressions, which often remain indelibly in the memories of the viewers because of the importance of the occasion. It is certainly not unreasonable to assume that a person who works all of his life to be thought of as a "good" *person* would not want to be remembered as a corpse.

In a similar vein, it is not safe to assume that our treatment of the dead in general, and funeral practices in particular, exist in their present forms solely because the American public wishes to ignore or deny death. Impermeable caskets, cosmetic embalming, and funeral wear all generate excellent financial returns to the funeral industry, as well as serve to justify the existence of such an industry. In an effort to generalize from the products and practices of the funeral industry to the American public, proponents of the death denial contention seem to make the implicit assumption that if the public did not wish to deny death, this very desire would affect a change in these customs and practices. The validity of this assumption is definitely questionable: These established methods, so profitable to the industry, could obviously be maintained despite the desires of the consumer, at least in the short run.

To illustrate the resistance to innovations which might narrow the profit margin, we look to an illuminating sequence of events which has recently transpired within the flower industry. Mitford has reported that from sixty to seventy percent of the flower industry's profits come from funeral-related flower sales. In the late 1950's, a number of people began adopting a practice which was a direct threat to this substantial profit source. Rather than sending flowers to funerals and the families of the "deceased," they contributed to charities in his memory. Soon many obituaries could be found ending with requests similar to "Please omit flowers. Memorial contributions to the   fund preferred." Needless to say, these "Please Omit", or "P.O.", notices were perceived as a threat by the flower industry, and they took deliberate measures to ensure that the public's wishes would not be met. First, funeral directors, who are generally responsible for placing the obituaries in the papers, were reminded that flowers played a key role in the "memory picture" which they were trying to create. It was argued that if this practice of "Please Omit" were to continue, the same general mental process which was operating to phase out the flowers would also generalize to the omission of expensive caskets, cosmetics, and many of the other practices and accessories which made the funeral business so profitable. Representatives of the flower industry maintained that, in fact, both industries were under the same criticism, and that together they could fight opposition more effectively.

The second tactic employed by the flower interests virtually forced the newspapers to adopt a policy of not accepting "P.O." notices. In 1957 as many as seventy-five to eighty-five percent of this nation's newspapers regularly carried such requests. In an attempt to curtail this practice, the Flower Information Council adopted the policy of increasing the amount spent on advertising in a given newspaper; when the paper came to be reliant on these funds, they characteristically sent a representative of the Council to suggest to the editors that they stop accepting "P.O." notices. So successful was this ploy and related tactics that by 1959 the executive secretary of the Society of American Florists was able to report that "241 cities had been visited by field men, and 199 newspapers had agreed to refrain using 'please omit' phrases."[25]

The reactions of the flower industry to the threat of innovation strongly suggests that the mere fact that a practice exists does not warrant the conclusion that it reflects the attitudes or desires of an entire society. Even when a practice or product is not desired or desirable the individuals who profit from it can find ways to ensure its continuance. Furthermore, unwanted funeral customs may persist even when not maintained or supported by vested economic interests. For example, Mitra tells of the trying ordeal he underwent in his native India in attempting to eliminate outmoded mourning customs which much of the population considered to be unhealthy, inconvenient, and unnecessary.[26] His efforts were largely unsuccessful, for the customs continued under their own momentum, despite the lack of popular support.

In line with the immediately preceding discussion, it should not be forgotten that while a person may reveal his denial of death through the use of euphemisms, these euphemisms are also

> ...the same familiar Madison Avenue language, with its peculiar adjectival range designed to anesthetize sales resistance to all sorts of products, [which have] seeped out into the funeral industry in a new and bizarre guise.[27]

Although the point being made here is a simple one, its importance is difficult to overestimate. It is unwarranted to assume that the mere existence of a culturally adopted custom necessarily implies a desire on the part of the participants in that culture for its presence and continuation. In spite of their frequent reliance upon this invalid assumption, however, proponents of the death denial argument are yet well grounded in their contention that Americans do not advocate sweeping changes in those practices which appear to reveal a denial of death's reality. Demands for revisions or reforms in these customs are neither loud nor constant from the general population; when changes *are* called for, the attack on present practices is ordinarily aimed at their expense or extravagance, not at the fact that they deny the existence of death.

In addition to the rather substantial evidence considered thus far, much of the daily routine of Americans can be interpreted as reflecting a basic death denial attitude. Americans, for example, often pride themselves on their sense of humor and frequently joke about death. Fulton and Geis claim that the use of humor in reference to death is characteristic of our society, and that the implementation of humor in this connection serves as "another manifestation of a general reluctance to accept its inevitability."[28] Previously, T. D. Eliot, the acknowledged pioneer of death research, had also noted that death was a frequent theme in American humor.[29] During the first few decades of this century, for example, jokes concerning death were told almost as frequently as those about sex. Eliot reasoned that jokes about death and about sex were psychologically analogous, since

> The joke is an expression from repression of an intolerable reality-experience which cannot be seriously faced. When the reality is upon us it ceases to be funny.[30]

Just as our jokes about death reflect our denial of the reality of death, so too does our characteristic reaction to death statistics. When the mass media inform us of the mounting death tolls in Vietnam or the number of automobile fatalities over a holiday weekend, we hear the figures, but react to them as numbers, not as deaths. Geoffrey Gorer argues that changed techniques in mass communications have made the denial of death in the form of callousness the only feasible reaction to the amount of misery, cruelty and death to which we are exposed.[31] It is quite inconceivable that one could react emotionally to every death to which he is exposed by the media and still remain sane, or, for that matter, have time to do anything else but emote.

Many other features of our experience mirror our denial of death. A study of modern art by Gottlieb shows that, with the exception of certain artists working at the end of the nineteenth century, contemporary artists have avoided using death as a subject to an astonishing degree. In contrast with other periods in which death was a frequent theme, entire groups and shcools of modern artists, both here and abroad, have avoided death in their works.[32] Wolfenstein's 1950 content analysis of American movies revealed that, while death is often found in our films, the way in which it is usually treated indicates a denial of its reality.[33] The vast majority of the movies which contained a death in the plot did not allow the audience to identify emotionally with the character who was to die. In those movies dealing specifically with murder, the victim was hardly ever known by the viewer to any significant degree and was never mourned openly by any of the friends or relatives who sought the killer. Death in the American film was generally cast as a catalyst to other action, not as a real event having emotional impact. It should be emphasized, however, that Wolfenstein's study dates back to 1950, and while its general findings are probably still quite valid, it is also likely that it is no longer as universally applicable as it once was. During the past decade we have witnessed great changes in the motion picture industry, including a fundamental shift away from the film which provides primarily superficial entertainment to that which is more thought-provoking, realistic, and emotionally intense. It is reasonable to assume that this shift has resulted in a more realistic treatment of death on the screen.

A final manifestation of the American denial of death to be considered here is the handling of death by American newspapers. Earlier in this chapter we noted the tendency of our society to segregate death and isolate it from our experience, a trait especially prevalent in our treatment of the aged, the dying, and the dead. Newspapers, similarly, have adopted a fairly universal policy of designating certain pages for obituaries and related articles (which are personal in their focus as opposed to the impersonal reporting of mass or tragic deaths, such those resulting from plane crashes, automobile accidents, and murders), thus ensuring that no mention of empathic death will invade other sections of the paper.[34] This segregation and isolation policy as it applies to newspapers allows the public to easily avoid contact with death in their reading and enables the press to avoid dealing extensively with what some readers might consider to be offensive subject matter. A more startling example of the newspapers' death denial is found in the fact that one of the leading United States newspapers, *The Christian Science Monitor*, did not until fairly recently even permit the word "death" to appear on its pages.[35]

Looking back, we find the American denial of death reflected in our newspapers, movies, modern art, reaction to death statistics, humor, varied funeral customs and practices, use of euphemisms for death, children's games and literature, and treatment of the aged and dying. We may conclude that those who contend that Americans deny the reality of death have indeed gathered considerable evidence and made their position appear well founded. In short, they have given us good reason to believe that Americans do, in fact, deny the eventuality and reality of their deaths and consistently avoid contacts with death which might make them less secure in their attitude of denial.

Herman Feifel has perhaps been the most insistent and vocal advocate of the denial position. He is quite representative of similarly inclined colleagues when he states that in the United States even a concern for death is taboo; that Americans are "compelled, in unhealthy measures, to internalize our thoughts and feelings, fears, and even hopes concerning death;" and that we run and hide from death, seeking refuge in the creation of a funeral industry which masks death by making the dead "life-like."[36] Feifel concludes that

> Even the words for death and dying are bypassed in much of everyday language by means of euphemism. It is not the disquieting 'I die,' but rather the anonymous 'one passes on,' 'one ends his days.' We 'exit,' 'cease,' become 'defunct' or 'demised,' but rarely die. The military makes death impersonal, and prevalent entertainment treats death not so much as a tragedy, but dramatic illusion.[37]

Reasons for American death denial

Several reasons may be offered to explain why Americans do not face death as an inevitability, but rather deny its reality. Americans appear to acquire and hold an attitude of death denial from a very early age. It will be recalled that American children exhibit this tendency in their games and fantasies. The child is also predisposed toward the denial of his own death because he is shielded from accurate information concerning death. As was discussed in Chapter One, American parents typically find it a most difficult matter to deal with, and, as a consequence, say almost nothing about it to their children. Further, the way is paved for the development and maintenance of a death denial attitude by the fact that American children so seldom come in contact with the dead and the dying. Margaret Mead has reported that, in contrast to Samoans, Americans

> ...[try] to protect their children from direct contact with and observation of death and the dead. In Samoa, 'all children had seen birth and death' and had seen many dead bodies'[38]

The difference in the amount of contact the respective groups of children had had with death and the dead seems quite natural in light of the differing mortality rates of the two societies. A low rate in a highly industrialized nation would tend to preclude much contact, whereas the Samoan rate would make contact there almost inevitable for the young. Regardless of the specific contributory factors, the lack of contact with and accurate information about death and the dead are important variables in the development of the attitude of death denial found in American children, for without "exposure," the notion of one's death is rendered virtually meaningless.

A second factor arising in childhood which is thought to carry over into adult denial is that the well-loved, non-rejected child in this society has a propensity to retain unconsciously the infantile certainty of his omnipotence. His feeling of invulnerability allows him to remain calm, for despite a vast array of facts to the contrary, his own death is not only not inevitable, it is not realistically possible. One thus handles death anxiety by denying the reality of one's death, which "...enables one to effectively isolate death from himself."[39]

In adults there are several reasons why death is denied. First, denying death apparently has a somewhat magical effect, for when one denies death he evidently feels that he is thereby causing death itself to vanish. This variety of magical thinking makes death "...not death at all, but ...rather a fictive experience."[40] Second, many Americans not only conceive of death as bad fortune and loss of life, but they also feel that it contains overtones of personal failure and loss of status and identity.[41] A society which places such a high value on success and at the same time defines death as a failure would tend to deny death's existence as it would deny the existence of any future failure. A third reason that might lead people to deny death could be "that the drive for life is so strong that the opposing objective experience cannot maintain itself."[42] That is, we want to live so badly that we cannot bring ourselves to believe that we will die. Finally, denial may in fact be a healthy and effective attitude toward one's death: While it is true that death is a fact of life, one may legitimately ask how much one can think realistically about his death and still live his life to the fullest. With much of life being hazardous, many desired experiences would be avoided were death not denied to some extent. Montaigne felt that denial of death was so healthy an attitude that everyone should adopt it. He argued:

> I have never seen any of my peasant neighbours give any thought to the question of how he would pass his last hour with dignity and assurance; nature has taught him not to think of death until it is at hand; and then he acquits himself with better grace than Aristotle, whom death does doubly oppress—once on its own account and once by his long premeditations.[43]

Thus, individual Americans may deny their own deaths because such denial is a healthier and more effective attitude for living life than is acceptance; because the will to live precludes perception of death; because death may be thought of as an unacceptable failure; because a person's denial of death is unconsciously believed to make death magically nonexistent; because one retains an infantile belief in his invulnerability and immortality; and/or because, as a child, the American seldom has contact with actual death or accurate information about death. At least one important question remains to be answered, however. Why might the vast majority of Americans, the American society, and American culture also respond with, reflect, or foster an attitude of death denial?

There seem to be several features of American life which make denial a very likely societal and cultural attitude. First, demographic changes accompanying the advance of modern medicine in the United States encourage the rejection of death, for the deaths of others, which might serve to remind us of our own impending deaths, are removed from our experience for most of our lives. As has been seen, death is becoming increasingly restricted to the aged, and they are customarily kept out of sight in nursing homes and retirement communities. When we do experience the death of a person with whom we are emotionally involved, it usually occurs in such a setting, which robs it of much of its impact; since the person who dies is usually elderly, it is more difficult to identify with his death. Thus, death remains unreal, its image barely sharpened by the vague contact recently experienced.

In addition to purely demographic considerations, denial of death in America is further facilitated by our modern family system, which relinquishes the role of caring for the dead and dying to professional functionaries. By so doing the family minimizes "...the average person's exposure to death and its disruption of the social process," and assures that no "...corpses interfere greatly with the mainstream of life."[44] Without the interference of death in one's life pattern, the denial of death becomes a natural and easily adopted attitude.

Moreover, the unparalleled American advance in science and technology quite readily leads to the belief that death can be eliminated in the same way that much illness and suffering have been eliminated. Most sickness has become "preventable and curable, and its companion, death, seemed equally vulnerable to our attack, an attack which was largely an elaborate denial."[45] While scientists cannot realistically predict or foresee the elimination of death in our lifetime, the United States has witnessed the discovery of cures for what were once incurable illnesses, and these remarkable successes have made for a certain faith in science's ultimate potential to "cure" death. If we are capable of believing that our science and technology can rid us of death, then surely we can quite as easily adopt the attitude that we will not die.

A final factor which may be relevant in explaining American death denial is suggested by the observations of Hans Morgenthau.[46] Morgenthau argues that earlier Americans could remove the stigma of death through a belief in the immortality of the person. While this immortality originally took a religious form, modern Americans have increasingly come to believe that what is human in them survives their bodily deaths. Thus, the contemporary American has made monuments testifying to his existence, created families which bear his name, erected tombstones which possess the flavor of eternity, had portraits done of him, planted trees, built houses, written poems, developed theories, composed music, invented machines, and made an infinite number of attempts to ensure his social immortality. Despite these elaborate ploys, however, he is denied even this more certain concept of immortality, for he lives in a nuclear age in which potential mass destruction is an established fact. This destruction would not only take his own life, but also all of its visible achievements. Similarly, a nuclear holocaust would also render the individual's death meaningless by stripping it of its uniqueness: Unlike conventional wars in which one could at least sacrifice his own life for his family's survival or for a cause, nuclear destruction would allow man to do neither, since his death would not be an act of volition in any sense. Thus, by virtue of his existence in a nuclear age, which deprives him of both social immortality and a meaningful death, the modern American is further predisposed toward death denial.

To summarize, American society and its culture seem quite congenial to an attitude of death denial fostered by the nuclear age, the characteristic faith in science and technology, the relinquishing of the care for the dead and dying by the family, and the demographic features of American death. The proponents of the death denial argument thus appear to be very well grounded in their assertion that Americans deny their own eventual deaths. Not only is there a substantial body of evidence which reflects an attitude of death denial in this society, but there is also good reason to believe that such an attitude is adopted logically and naturally, and is, perhaps, the only attitude suited to the realities of American life and death.

Although we have heard an impressive case favoring the death denial position, we should refrain from jumping to premature conclusions regarding American attitudes toward death until we have heard the arguments, evidence, and research findings of those who hold the opposite view in the acceptance-denial controversy. Those serious students of death research who contend that Americans accept the eventuality and reality of their deaths are no less insistent that their position is the only reasonable and correct one. In Chapter Four we examine the arguments of the proponents of the death acceptance contention in light of the supporting evidence and rationale.

NOTES

1. P. Tillich, "The Eternal Now," in Herman Feifel (ed.), *The Meaning of Death,* New York: McGraw-Hill Book Company, Inc., 1959, pp. 31-32.

2. C. W. Wahl, "The Fear of Death," in Robert Fulton (ed.), *Death and Identity,* New York: John Wiley and Sons, Inc., 1965, p. 58.
3. W. Bromberg and P. Schilder, "Death and Dying," *Psychoanalytic Review,* 1933, 20, pp. 142-143.
4. Feifel, *op. cit.,* XIX.
5. Wahl, *op. cit.,* p. 62.
6. *Ibid.,* p. 62.
7. R. Kastenbaum, "Time and Death in Adolescence," in Feifel, *op. cit.,* p. 104.
8. L. Pound, "American Euphemisms for Dying, Death and Burial: An Anthology," *American Speech,* 1936, 11, p. 195.
9. J. Mitford, *The American Way of Death,* New York: Simon and Schuster, 1963.
10. R. Fulton and G. Geis, "Death and Social Values," in Fulton, *op. cit.,* p. 69.
11. A. E. Christ, "Attitudes Toward Death Among a Group of Acute Geriatric Psychiatric Patients," *Journal of Gerontology,* 1961, 16, p. 59.
12. C. Driver, "The Great Unmentionable," *Atlas,* August, 1965, 10, p. 114.
13. Feifel, *op. cit.,* XIV.
14. Fulton, *op. cit.,* p. 4.
15. R. Blauner, "Death and the Social Structure," *Psychiatry,* 1966, 29, p. 385.
16. J. K. Owen, *Modern Concepts of Hospital Administration,* Philadelphia: Saunders Publishing Company, 1962, p. 304.
17. Blauner, *op. cit.,* p. 386.
18. R. A. Kalish, "Aged and the Dying Process: The Inevitable Decision," *Journal of Social Issues,* 1965, 21, p. 88.
19. *Ibid.,* p. 88.
20. *Ibid.,* p. 88.
21. Mitford, *op. cit.,* p. 14.
22. *Ibid.,* p. 16.
23. Fulton and Geis, *op. cit.,* pp. 68-69.
24. Mitford, *op. cit.,* p. 14.
25. *Ibid.,* pp. 87-92.
26. D. N. Mitra, "Mourning Customs and Modern Life in Bengal," *American Journal of Sociology,* 1947, 52, pp. 309-311.
27. Mitford, *op. cit.,* pp. 13-14.
28. Fulton and Geis, *op. cit.,* p. 69.
29. T. D. Eliot, "A Step Toward the Social Psychology of Bereavement," *Journal of Abnormal and Social Psychology,* 1933, 27, p. 380.
30. *Ibid.,* p. 380.
31. G. Gorer, *Death, Grief and Mourning,* New York: Doubleday, 1965, p. 131.
32. C. Gottlieb, "Modern Art and Death," in Feifel, *op. cit.,* pp. 157-188.
33. M. Wolfenstein and N. Leets, *Movies: A Psychological Study,* Glencoe, Ill.: The Free Press, 1950, pp. 233-242.
34. Fulton and Geis, *op. cit.,* p. 100.
35. Feifel, *op. cit.,* pp. 115-116.
36. H. Feifel, "Death," *The Encyclopedia of Mental Health,* 1963, Vol. 2, p. 448.
37. *Ibid.,* p. 448.
38. Mead, cited in Fulton and Geis, *op. cit.,* p. 68.
39. Wahl, *op. cit.,* p. 61.

40. *Ibid.,* p. 58.
41. Feifel, "Death," *op. cit.,* p. 449.
42. Bromberg and Schilder, *op. cit.,* p. 184.
43. Quoted in E. Geiringer, "Fear of Death," *Spectator,* August 8, 1952, 189, p. 180.
44. Blauner, *op. cit.,* p. 384.
45. A. M. Kasper, "The Doctor and Death," in Feifel, *The Meaning of Death, op. cit.,* p. 259.
46. H. J. Morgenthau, "Death in the Nuclear Age," *Commentary,* 1961, 32, pp. 231-239.

Chapter Four

The American Acceptance of Death

No man enjoys the true taste of life but he who is willing and ready to quit it.

Seneca

It is the duty then of a thinking man to be neither superficial, nor impatient, nor yet contemptuous in his attitude toward death, but to await it as one of the operations of Nature which he will have to undergo.

Marcus Aurelius

Numerous interested scholars have not been persuaded by the evidence and rationale considered in the preceding chapter. Quite to the contrary, a significant proportion of them contend that Americans exhibit attitudinal acceptance of the inevitability of death. Rather than denying the reality of their own deaths, Americans are thought to actively accept this eventuality and to live their lives with the realization that they must indeed die. Proponents of the death acceptance argument generally concede that Americans fear death, but maintain that they cope with this fear by meeting death head on. Furthermore, the intensity of the American's fear is thought to be diminished by the "understanding" of death he attains through careful and rational thought and contemplation.

Typifying this counterposition is the argument advanced by Talcott Parsons, who, in May of 1963, published a working paper containing a clear articulation of the death acceptance hypothesis.[1] Parsons' article, which apparently caught the attention of a number of leading students of death attitude research, embodied the contention that the American attitude toward death had undergone a radical transformation from denial to acceptance.[2]

Parsons explicitly reveals his disputation of the denial argument in the introduction to his paper:

A widely current belief which seems to be open to *criticism* is the view that American society is characterized by a kind of *'denial'* of the reality of death. Phenomena in the practice of undertaking–the dressing of the corpse in ordinary clothes, the use of cosmetics, the very special concern with the impermeability of coffins–are all cited as evidence.[3] (italics ours)

Parsons' reasoning, stated briefly and syllogistically, is as follows:

(a) ...American society has institutionalized the values of science to a high degree.

(b) ...a certain realism in facing the facts of the world is characteristic of the scientific attitude.

(c) It would seem, therefore, to be anomalous that such a society would be characterized by a fundamental attitude [denial] which is so drastically at variance with that of science.[4]

Parsons thus argues that the scientific-rational orientation of contemporary United States society produces an atmosphere in which attitudinal acceptance of death becomes the modal view, and denial of death, a deviant response. According to Parsons, this remarkable transformation of attitudes is primarily the result of advances in modern medicine as well as the concomitant demographic changes in the age structure of society.[5] Medical advances have created a situation where the traditional association between death and suffering has become more and more tenuous. With the continued weakening of this once inexorable relationship, the fact of death apparently becomes more easily accepted.[6] Further, and even more importantly, with the greatly decreased incidence of "premature" or early death due to natural causes, death is no longer viewed as adventitious as it once was. These factors put the problem of the meaning of death as "the termination of a normal life cycle in what is probably a new state of relative purity in human experience."[7] In short, as death rates have declined dramatically and as the average expectation of life has markedly increased, death has come increasingly to be viewed as the natural completion of the life cycle, an inevitable occurrence of old age. Parsons bolsters his claim by arguing that

Combined with this demographic fact [lack of premature death] is the failure of the maximum span of human life to increase. This underlines the inevitability of death, and though it does not fix its time precisely, it narrows the range of its probable occurrence; for example, for people over 80 it is quite clear that they cannot have many more years to live.[8]

It is therefore quite natural and rational for the modern American to accept the inevitability of death, for it has come to be viewed as inescapable in old age. Our contacts with the aged serve to remind us of the eventuality of our own deaths, and, since the aged are coming to constitute an ever-increasing proportion of the total population, our awareness of death is made more acute and the acceptance of death more compelling. We turn now to consider the evidence for the contention that acceptance is the modal American attitude toward death and that,

> To the extent that this normal orientation prevails in American society, the individual is expected to face up to death in realistic terms, and his bereaved are expected to do their 'grief work' quickly and privately...[9]

Evidence in support of the death acceptance argument

Strong support for the acceptance hypothesis has been provided by the findings of a sample survey of a cross-section of the United States adult population, conducted by Riley and Goldwater in conjunction with the National Opinion Research Center of the University of Chicago.[10] It was discovered that over eighty percent of the respondents felt that one should not ignore (deny) death, but rather should "try to make some plans about it." Further, while few people had made wills or made funeral or cemetery arrangements, eighty percent of those questioned had purchased life insurance, and fifty percent had made a point of talking about their deaths with those closest to them.[11] In light of these findings, Riley concluded that

> ...it seems clearly to be the case that the American people are inclined not only to talk about death, but also to include a note of practical realism in the meaning they attach to it.[12]

It is difficult to place as much confidence in this conclusion as Riley seems to exhibit in formulating and advancing it. While the responses obtained do suggest realistic acceptance of death, the validity and reliability of overt questioning techniques in death attitude research are particularly problematical.[13] It is well to keep in mind that "We should not be misled by an avowed acceptance of one's death or even resignation," for one is not likely to answer that he denies the existence of an obvious reality.[14] Furthermore, death denial may operate primarily on the level of the subconscious, thereby precluding its overt revelation even for those subjects attempting to give honest and accurate representations of their attitudes.

Of the several findings of this study, the fact that eighty percent of the sample had purchased life insurance may possess a reasonable degree of validity as an indicator of attitudinal acceptance. While it is likely that the magnitude of life insurance purchase may be spuriously inflated by such extraneous factors as effective advertising and social pressures, the extremely high percentage of policy holders would indeed seem to be attributable to an acceptance of death's inevitability. For the advertising to be effective, those individuals constituting the potential market must be aware that they will die; without a fundamental attitude of acceptance, even the most glamorous life insurance plan having optimum benefits and lowest cost would fail to attract a substantial clientele. Too, Americans make many decisions on the basis of economic considerations, and life insurance is a costly proposition. It is therefore not unreasonable to venture the contention that Americans would not spend the vast sums which support our life insurance industry merely as "protection" from a death which they did not entertain as a real possibility, especially in light of the myriad other items and services on which the money might well be spent. The point is simply this: People do not buy auto insurance if they own no cars and, similarly, they probably would not buy life insurance if they had no belief in the fact that they will die.

Interestingly, much of the additional evidence which may be advanced in support of the acceptance hypothesis is to be found by examining many of the same types of phenomena and behaviors cited in support of attitudinal denial of death. The use of euphemisms for 'death' is a case in point. It may be argued, for example, that the very fact that we talk about death, even euphemistically, is indicative of acceptance. Furthermore, many such euphemisms function to underline the reality of death by emphasizing rather than hiding its more crass and morbid aspects. Graphic descriptions of death are conveyed by many popular euphemisms, some of which are: "breathed his last," "met his end," "clasped the cold embrace of death," "laid under the sod (or in the cold ground)," "bit the dust," "sleeps the sleep that knows no waking," "departed this life," "kicked the bucket," "put to bed with a shovel," "grounded for good," "made a stiff," "croaked," and "went home feet first."[15]

Other indications of acceptance of death are discovered in entertainment and art forms. As early as the 1920's, for example, European authors began treating death in vivid and realistic terms. Perhaps one of the earliest to do so was Zweig, who even noted at the end of a novel written in 1928 that when a sergeant was shot, "his bowels discharged excrement;" in that period, as Kaufmann has argued, "it took some courage" for an author "to disregard propriety and admit that some, when shot, will fill their pants."[16] American authors have also tended to follow this trend as is evident in the works of Hemingway, dos Passos, and Faulkner. In the preceding chapter it was noted that American movies are also dealing with death in increasingly revealing and realistic terms. In fact, some have argued that American acceptance of death in the entertainment media seems to have reached a point of morbid preoccupation, testified to by the marked degree of violence shown on television and in the movies, heavy sales of "horror films" and "horror comic books," and "the thousands of ill written paperback books on the horror of war and concentration camps."[17]

Studies of the ill and dying also lend credence to the view that Americans accept death. For example, it has been found that terminally ill patients accept and integrate information from their physicians that they will die in the near future, provided that they are not told too abruptly.[18] These patients have apparently developed an attitude of death acceptance earlier in life and, when they learn of the approximate time of death, find death not prohibitively difficult to accept. In addition, whatever the cause of death, "we can say, by and large, that the man who is about to die has made peace with himself."[19] These findings are at least indirectly supportive of Parsons' contention that the recognition of death's inevitability is associated with attitudinal acceptance.

One of the most persuasive indicants of acceptance is provided by the simple fact that research and discussions on the topic of death are now being conducted openly, without the fear of condemnation or reprisal. Not so long ago this book could not have been written, or if written, would not have been extensively read, because of public and academic disapproval of the subject matter. Both the authors and the readers would have been typed as social deviants of peculiar and morbid perversions. In contemporary American society, however, there is greater "intellectual and effective permissiveness" that reflects acceptance of the reality of death and, "at long last one can find a few genuine indications of straightforeward discussions and investigations of death..."[20]

As was noted above, evidence for the acceptance hypothesis emanates from many of the same sources which have been congenial to serious advocates of the denial contention. This parallel finds its way into the behavior patterns which Americans exhibit in their reaction to and treatment of the already dead, namely, in the funeral industry, in burial customs, and in bereavement practices. First, the sheer size of the American funeral industry is believed to force a public acceptance of death. This country's funeral profession is extremely proud of the fact that

> ...there is not a person in the continental limits of the United States who is more than two hours away from a licensed funeral director and embalmer in case of need. That's one even the fire-fighting apparatus of our country cannot match.[21]

While it is quite likely that we may often ride past a funeral home and ignore it completely, or at least not wholly realize its significance, it is also quite likely that there are many people who, on several occasions in their lives, are strongly reminded of the inevitability of their fate upon seeing a funeral home. Similarly, viewing a funeral procession–the limousine decked out with flowers, the hearse following with the corpse, the line of cars with headlights on and filled with mourners–also serves to remind us that someday we will be the point of interest in such a procession. Cemeteries, obituaries, and memorial church services further compel us to accept the reality that we, too, must die.

In the preceding chapter it was held that the funeral service reflects a denial of death, since in its modern American form death is hidden by the attempts to make the corpse appear alive–by cosmetic embalming, life-like attire, exposure in a "slumber room," and the like. Antithetically, these same practices have been said to mirror a strong and unambiguous acceptance of death by compelling mourners and onlookers to acknowledge the existence of death. The funeral director, it is held, must make a living from his profession, and

> ...if he is to justify his role as an important functionary in death, must focus attention upon the body. Display of the corpse, of course, forces attention upon death itself, but also allows a society with a growing repression of it to deal more comfortably with reality by presenting it in the most favorable form available.[22]

Because the funeral director must justify his role and because he desires to impress his client and possible future clients with his handling of the deceased, the corpse is almost always laid out in such a fashion as to focus attention upon it. Light is directed at the casket, the flowers are arranged to lead the straying eye back to the body, and if the room in which the corpse is displayed is equipped with chairs, they are placed so that everyone faces the casket–the funeral director's finished product. In short, the visiting room is arranged and the funeral planned in a manner which focuses attention on death and demands an acceptance of its reality. Funerals are memorable occasions which do not allow the participants to either forget or deny the reality of the death which has led to the sequence of events they have experienced: those viewing the body are left with an indelible impression; the bereaved are expected to remain with the corpse to greet mourners; those participating in the funeral are impressed with its pageantry and accompanying emotional displays; relatives must pay for the funeral, the cemetery, and other related accessories, and they often must sacrifice to do so. Constant reminders of death's reality to those involved, all of these individual impressions are caused by a single passing. The ultimate result of such experiences is that,

> When a family has spent three days, as is the case in most Christian communities, or seven days, as is the general Jewish practice, in accepted mourning procedures, the reality of the death of the body cannot be easily denied. The 'viewing of the remains,' the visits of friends and family, the rituals of the community and religious institutions that confront the mourner day after day,

gradually bring the consciousness of death to all levels of being and make it difficult for fantasies and illusions to develop in thoughts or feelings of the individual.[23]

Thus, although Americans typically experience the death of one close to them only rarely in their lives, this exposure leaves no room for doubting that death is real and must be accepted. Even after the funeral and burial have taken place, the bereaved are not allowed to forget the fact of death. The affairs of the deceased must be attended to, his will executed, his clothes and other personal reminders of his life cared for. Those who come to console and to make the burden easier to bear force further acceptance of death's reality and finality, for this "rather tortuous process" of trying to talk to people who attempt to console (but often do not know how) reinforces the consciousness that death is universal, real, inevitable, and permanent. We are therefore compelled to accept the fact that someday others will grieve for us as we have grieved for the deceased.

Our characteristic manner of grieving, and of consoling those who grieve, also reflect a societal acceptance of death, for an American is expected to come quickly to grips with the reality of another person's death, accept it, and then return to normal life. In its bereavement practices our society manifests an

> ...expectation of stoical acceptance of death. The expression of grief or sympathy for a death is limited to time and place. The dramaturgy of death moves inexorably to a conclusion–often only three days. Within one week one is expected to be back on the job.[24]

This tendency toward stoical death acceptance as evidenced by contemporary bereavement practices seems analogous to the British situation, where "...giving way to grief is stigmatized as morbid, unhealthy [and] demoralizing..."[25] One is expected to view death as a very real and natural part of existence, and, as a result, "mourning is treated as if it were weakness, self-indulgence, a reprehensible bad habit, instead of a psychological necessity."[26]

Additional support for the acceptance hypothesis stems from the increasing public disapproval of many of the practices of the American funeral industry, practices which are said to reflect and perpetuate death denial. When Roul Tunley published an article in the June 17, 1961 issue of the *Saturday Evening Post* entitled "Can You Afford to Die?", the editors were quite astonished by their readers' responses; rarely had the public reacted so strongly to any of their articles. Within three months, six thousand letters were written by people from all walks of life, criticizing the ornateness and expense of practices designed to shield them from death's reality.[27] These irate individuals apparently did not value

such techniques as "cosmetic embalming," or the numerous services offered by the "grief therapist;" neither did they wish to spend their money
on fantasy. This discontent with current funeral practices is also manifested in the growing membership rolls of funeral and memorial associations which are concerned with planning simple, reasonably priced and
dignified funerals. They have increased from their original constituency
of primarily the "more sophisticated elements of the population" to a
wider and more heterogeneous membership, which has "skyrocketed."[28]
Although we cannot be certain to what extent the American people as
a whole disapproves of those funeral industry practices which deny
the reality of death, nor to what degree such disapproval might be stimulated by a fundamental attitude of acceptance, the evidence is indeed
suggestive.

Taken altogether, so suggestive have been research findings and more
casual observations of everyday American life, that several interested
scholars have been persuaded that death acceptance constitutes a vital
force in the determination of behavior, and that such an attitude has a
profound impact on the phenomenon of death itself. Even Herman Feifel,
whose work classifies him as one of the most forceful and articulate proponents of the denial hypothesis, has argued that many of man's greatest
advances stem from a fundamental attitude of acceptance. Since some
men have accepted the fact that they must eventually die, he reasons, they
have been willing to sacrifice their lives prematurely so that mankind
might benefit.[29] In Feifel's words,

> This condition [acceptance of death] has, in large measure, been responsible
> for many of the advances of our science, medicine, and technology. Not until
> man overcame the fear of death could he permit himself to be bitten voluntarily
> by a mosquito infested with yellow fever germs, sail the seven seas, master the
> art of flying, and tomorrow this condition will bring into our ken knowledge of
> vast new worlds of space.[30]

The motive force of death acceptance has also been recognized by other
writers, but as harmful rather than beneficial. Herbert Marcuse has discussed the "sinister aspect" of the death acceptance attitude, when death
acceptance assumes a morbid and abnormal character. He contends that
this sinister aspect appears in stories drawn from ancient times about
mothers who

> ...delighted in the sacrifice of their sons on the battlefields; in the more recent
> letters of mothers who assured the killers of their sons of their forgiveness; in
> the stoic indifference with which... [people] live near atomic testing grounds
> and take war for granted.[31]

The sinister aspect of death acceptance reveals clearly that this attitude has dysfunctional as well as eufunctional implications. In any event, it must be conceded that the acceptance attitude constitutes an important force in the molding of behavior and the course of human events.

Reasons for American death acceptance

The rationale for American death acceptance requires significantly less elaboration than was true of our consideration of the rationale for the denial attitude, since the explanatory arguments are so plainly consistent with the accepted canons of western logic. That is, an American attitude of death acceptance seems quite natural, logical, and realistic in view of the fact that death is indeed universal and permanent. We must all die sooner or later, and the hypothesis that Americans accept this fact appears hardly far-fetched. This conclusion is rendered particularly compelling in light of Talcott Parsons' argument, cited at the beginning of this chapter: the acceptance attitude is entirely consonant with and bolstered by the scientific-rational orientation which so permeates the very fiber of contemporary American society. Death, which has become increasingly dissociated from suffering, is therefore conceived as a natural and inevitable concomitant of aging.

Several other explanations for American death acceptance have been advanced. For example, it has been argued that acceptance of one's death may be a crucial product of the maturation process, and that it constitutes an absolute necessity for normal and adaptive living. William E. Hocking, an advocate of this position, has pointed out that human maturity "brings along with it a recognition of limit, which is a notable advance of self knowledge."[32] Death, the absolute limit to our existence, should be recognized as such by the mature adult. In fact, the way we live our lives implies and even necessitates this maturity. If we cannot accept our deaths and are, therefore, commanded by an inescapable desire to live,

> ...the everyday risks of living, e.g., driving downtown, taking an airplane trip, losing one's guard in sleeping, become extravagent folly. Life is not genuinely our own until we renounce it.[33]

Death acceptance may result, not only from maturity, but also from a sense of fulfillment. In the preceding chapter it was noted that the individual American may deny his own death if he has not accomplished his valued goals, the attainment of which is intimately interrelated with and necessary to his self-esteem. In accordance with this contention, Riley adds that if a person has attained his important goals, and thereby feels fulfilled, he is more ready and able to accept his death.[34] Under these circumstances individuals tend to accept death because they see it as a kind of "curtain on a well acted play," or because death means personal fulfillment in other ways, such as reunions with loved ones already dead, resolution of conflicts, cessation of troubles, or a gateway to a new life.[35]

The arguments cited in support of the reasonableness of an acceptance attitude are not always as positive as those just discussed. It has been suggested, for example, that people often accept death because they are ignorant of death's full meaning (as is often the case with children), or because such acceptance may represent an escape from reality as a product of anxiety neurosis.[36] Finally, people often accept death because, while it may be "A painful, horrible, violent and unwelcome event," they feel their lives to have been "...even more painful than death."[37]

We conclude this chapter by emphasizing the uncertainties and contradictions which currently characterize our knowledge of American attitudes toward death. The antithetical hypotheses of attitudinal acceptance and attitudinal denial of death are both apparently equally well supported by the available evidence. Furthermore, each appears consistent with other facets of American life and death, natural and inevitable reactions to the contemporary American situation. The logical reconstructions of both arguments are parallel and, in fact, it is frequently possible to examine and find support for each position in the very same practices, customs, and varieties of behavior. The opposing positions seem to be of virtually equal strength, yet they contradict each other at every turn. While we may have arrived at a slightly better understanding of the ways in which Americans view death, as well as an appreciation of what we have labeled the 'acceptance-denial controversy,' we are clearly not much closer to a resolution of the controversy than we were when we embarked upon this venture. Having read and even pondered the preceding evidence and rationale, the reader may very well find himself somewhat confused, and may perhaps feel that the only certainty concerning death is contained in the Viennese saying, "So many people now die who never died before." Indeed, Robert Fulton summarizes well what we have discovered thus far when he states that, in terms of social scientific knowledge, "the status of death attitudes is at best ambiguous..."[38]

The intent of the remaining chapters is twofold. On the one hand, we shall be concerned with explaining why this state of ambiguity, uncertainty, and contradiction prevails, and why the acceptance-denial controversy has developed. On the other hand, we shall pursue and ultimately suggest a resolution to the acceptance-denial controversy.

NOTES

1. T. Parsons, "Death in American Society: A Brief Working Paper," *American Behavioral Scientist,* 1963, 6, pp. 61-65.
2. *Ibid.* See, for example, Riley's discussion of the theoretical and empirical significance of Parsons' position in J. W. Riley, Jr., "Death and Bereavement," *International Encyclopedia of the Social Sciences,* 1968, Vol. 4, p. 22.
3. Parsons, *op. cit.,* p. 61.
4. *Ibid.,* p. 63.
5. *Ibid.,* pp. 62-63.
6. *Ibid.,* p. 62.
7. *Ibid.,* p. 62.
8. *Ibid.,* p. 63.
9. Riley, *op. cit.,* p. 22.
10. Reported in J. W. Riley, Jr., "Contemporary Society and the Institution of Life Insurance," *Journal of the American Society of Chartered Life Underwriters,* 1964, 18, pp. 93-103.
11. Riley, "Death and Bereavement," *op. cit.,* pp. 23-24.
12. Riley, "Contemporary Society and the Institution of Life Insurance," *op. cit.,* p. 102.
13. For example, see our discussion in Chapter Five.
14. J. C. Rheingold, *The Mother, Anxiety and Death,* Boston: Little, Brown and Company, 1967, pp. 40-41.
15. L. Pound, "American Euphemisms for Dying, Death and Burial: An Anthology," *American Speech,* 1936, 11, pp. 196-199.
16. W. Kaufmann, "Existentialism and Death," in Herman Feifel (ed.), *The Meaning of Death,* New York: McGraw-Hill Book Company, Inc., 1959, p. 51.
17. G. Gorer, *Death, Grief and Mourning,* New York: Doubleday, 1965, p. 132.
18. H. Feifel, "Attitudes Toward Death in Some Normal and Mentally Ill Populations," in Feifel, *op. cit.,* p. 125.
19. A. A. Hutschnecker, "Personality Factors in Dying Patients," in *ibid.,* pp. 247-248.
20. E. S. Shneidman, "Orientations Toward Death: A Vital Aspect of the Study of Lives," in Robert White (ed.), *The Study of Lives,* New York: Atherton Press, 1963, p. 201.
21. Cited in J. Mitford, *The American Way of Death,* New York: Simon and Schuster, 1963, p. 66.
22. R. Fulton and G. Geis, "Death and Social Values," in Robert Fulton (ed.), *Death and Identity,* New York: John Wiley and Sons, Inc., 1965, p. 73.
23. E. N. Jackson, "Grief and Religion," in Feifel, *The Meaning of Death, op. cit.,* p. 220.
24. R. Fulton, "The Sacred and the Secular: Attitudes of the American Public toward Death, Funerals and Funeral Directors," in Fulton, *op. cit.,* p. 101.
25. Gorer, *op. cit.,* pp. 130-131.
26. *Ibid.,* pp. 130-131.
27. Mitford, *op. cit.,* p. 20.

28. *Ibid.,* p. 20.
29. Actually, Feifel never proves that acceptance of death is the cause of these advances, but merely reasons that this is the case. It seems equally logical to argue that an attitude of death denial could also stimulate such "progress." For example, to consider the quotation that follows, one may be willing to be bitten by the disease-bearing mosquito because he refuses to believe that he will die–he denies his death.
30. Feifel, "Attitudes Toward Death in Some Normal and Mentally Ill Populations," *op. cit.,* p. 125.
31. H. Marcuse, "The Ideology of Death," in Feifel, *The Meaning of Death, op. cit.,* pp. 74-75.
32. Noted in H. Feifel, "Death," *The Encyclopedia of Mental Health,* 1963, Vol. 2, p. 430.
33. *Ibid.,* p. 430.
34. Riley, "Death and Bereavement," *op. cit.,* p. 23.
35. Feifel, "Death," *op. cit.,* p. 438.
36. H. Becker and D. K. Bruner, "Attitudes Toward Death and the Dead and Some Possible Causes of Ghost Fear," *Mental Hygiene,* 1931, 15, p. 829.
37. Marcuse, *op. cit.* p. 69.
38. R. L. Fulton, "Attitudes Toward Death: A Discussion," *Journal of Gerontology,* 1961, 16, p. 64.

PART THREE

TOWARD A
SUGGESTED RESOLUTION

Chapter Five

Methodological Problems
in Death Attitude Research

> *In listening to these papers this morning one thing stands out above everything else, and that is the contradictory nature of their findings.*
>
> Robert Fulton commenting on papers presented at the Fifth Congress of the International Association of Gerontology on Aged Attitudes Toward Death, 1961.

While the above quotation by Robert Fulton referred to studies concerned specifically with the death attitudes of the aged, his astute observations on the contradictory nature of their findings is quite applicable to the research conducted on death attitudes in general–a point sufficiently illustrated, and indeed dramatized, throughout our systematic examination of the acceptance-denial controversy. The objective of the present chapter is to advance a partial explanation for the contradictory findings of death attitude research in terms of both general and specific methodological weaknesses which have plagued this particular area of scientific inquiry. It is hoped that the reader will thereby acquire an understanding of some of the more salient problems inherent in the methods and techniques currently employed to gain valid and reliable insights into and information about American death attitudes, and that he will thus be made aware of one of the main reasons why the findings of both the acceptance and denial positions have proved to be so contradictory and, consequently, inconclusive. It should be noted that many of the methodological problems discussed in this chapter plague the field of sociology as a whole, but they are particularly problematical as regards such a sensitive and emotion-laden field of inquiry as death attitudes. We turn immediately to the task at hand.

General methodological shoddiness

Put quite simply, the first methodological explanation of why research in this field has yielded such glaring discrepancies is that many of the research efforts have been logically and/or empirically shoddy. This general methodological shoddiness is not necessarily due either to problems which are inherent in the subject matter or to the lack of available sophisticated techniques, but rather is a function of a most astounding paucity of rigor which may be spotted quickly by the critical reader. The methodologically sensitized reader is further annoyed by the patently unsound methods used in arriving at supposedly factual findings which exhibit questionable validity and reliability. While the tendency toward methodological shoddiness in the area of death research is quite prevalent, we can consider but a few typical examples here.

Alexander and Alderstein have observed that the several studies undertaken by various researchers in an effort to determine the nature and degree of children's emotional involvement with death have reported an extremely large variety of types and degrees of involvement.[1] While some studies have reputedly found salient attitudes of acceptance and reality orientation toward death, for example, others claim to have discovered staunch denial and morbid concern. In reaching these conclusions, however, researchers reporting both types of findings reveal a decided lack of methodological sophistication. Alexander and Alderstein have argued that,

> With regard to affective arousal, the indicators used by the investigators were gross. They were mainly clinical judgments of play, fantasy, and discussion. The data did not lend themselves easily to quantification or to reliability or validity checks.[2]

As a result of these kinds of deficiencies, we are placed in the uncomfortable position of having to rely upon conclusions which are based primarily on what the various researchers subjectively interpret certain activities or statements to represent, such interpretations having little demonstrable empirical support. Similarly, the lack of appropriate quantification and suitable checks on validity and reliability detract significantly from the potential credibility of the findings.

Another example of methodological weakness is provided by reference to Nagy's study dealing with the stages of death attitude formation in children.[3] Nagy's findings were cited in Chapter One in connection with the development of attitudes toward death, despite the severe limitations imposed by her discovery procedures. Since her study population included only children residing in Budapest, her ability to render meaningful generalizations is obviously seriously curtailed. Further, and more importantly, she offers no statistical analysis, providing only sample quotations to support her conclusions, and giving the reader no indication of how representative the remarks might be. Similarly, no information is given concerning the level of confidence with which one might predict general behavior patterns based on her findings and conclusions. The inconsistency of her data gathering techniques also poses crucial difficulties. Children of ages five through nine years were required to draw pictures with "death" in them, while the older children were asked to write compositions with a death theme. It should be noted that drawing places a great restriction on the way thoughts may be expressed, especially in young children. One has only to imagine the difficulty a child would have in drawing death *without* personifying it. This point is particularly cogent in light of Nagy's reported finding that younger (as opposed to older) children reveal a tendency to personify death in their thoughts. However, because of this inconsistency of technique, it is obviously quite possible that the reputed differences in thoughts about death could be a function of the varying research methods rather than, as hypothesized, a function of age. Finally, as Gardner noted,

> It is unfortunately true that Nagy's material is limited in depth and cultural perspective. [Nagy] does not seem to be aware that her data depend in any serious degree upon historical, sociocultural or specific conditions.[4]

Becker's earlier study of death attitudes relies solely on the works of such fiction writers as Shakespeare, Dickens, and Tennyson in quest of its objectives.[5] While this kind of literary technique might conceivably be useful in gaining insights into a potential range of attitudes or ideal typical attitudinal types, it should obviously not be employed in the determination of attitudes held by the man on the street. Although poets, novelists and playwrights have often displayed astute psychological and sociological imaginations, their contributions have been at best stimulants to more systematically inclined thinkers.

One final example should make still clearer the general methodological shoddiness characterizing attitudinal research on death. Recently, Fulton set out to investigate American attitudes toward death by distributing paper and pencil questionnaires to randomly selected households from urban areas.[6] Although the majority of Americans do currently reside in areas designated as urban, one is perplexed by Fulton's omission of rural householders. This deficiency in his sample frame casts an aura of doubt on the representativeness of his respondents. Further, and even more importantly, while over 10,000 questionnaires were originally sent out, his working sample consisted of the 1,264 (approximately 12%) which were returned. As is well known, the potential bias inherent in an 88% sample mortality rate is so serious as to render any findings virtually meaningless. In this regard, Fulton provides us with reason to suspect a strong area bias, for the indicated that the bulk of the instruments *not* returned were from the east and west coast areas.[7] Furthermore, it is quite probable that individuals taking the time to fill out and return the form possessed certain non-random characteristics, such as strong opinions on the subject or recent contact with death. Thus, the sample which was supposed to be representative of the American population was in actuality composed of urban, non-coastal householders possessing and unknowable quantity and quality of potentially relevant non-random characteristics, and constituting but 12% of the original sample.

In addition to Fulton's problems with sampling technique, a number of other potentially biasing factors can be noted within his study. For example, the questionnaires were sent out with cover letters explaining the purpose of the study; this explanation could very well have had an effect on the responses obtained. Fulton makes no mention of any attempts to check on the probable effects of the cover letter. The investigator evidently assumed, moreover, that the respondents could verbalize their attitudes toward death (an unwarranted assumption, for reasons presented later in this chapter). Finally, he neglected to indicate how the questionnaires were coded, tabulated or organized. In short, the general lack of rigor evident in this study makes questionable its descriptive and explanatory utility.

With research relying on the kinds of methodological inadequacies exhibited in the preceding examples, the proliferation of contradictory findings should come as no surprise. Obviously, there are a number of serious students of death research (such as Alexander and Alderstein, Greenberger, Kalish, Rheingold, and Sudnow) who are quite sophisticated methodologically, critical of their own procedures, and well aware of the limits to the validity of their claims. Unfortunately, however, they seem to constitute a minority in the area of death research.

Investigator bias

The second major methodological problem which plagues the field is that of the researcher *unknowingly* influencing the eventual findings of his study because of some preexisting bias. The term 'bias' is used here in Kaplan's sense to mean "adherence to values of such a kind or in such a way as to interfere with scientific objectivity."[8] An investigator, then, could hold a bias which would predispose him toward the misinterpretations of the meanings of certain behaviors. For example, because of an early or unusual experience with death, he might be biased so strongly in the direction of one set of values regarding death that he simply could not recognize behavior as exhibiting different or contrary values.

A number of serious students of death research hold what may be labeled a *cultural shock bias.* Having been socialized in one culture and having developed its characteristic form of ethnocentrism, they are "shocked" when exposed to the contrasting values and attitudes extant in another culture. This culture shock almost necessarily precludes an entirely objective analysis. The judgment of ethnographers has apparently been markedly affected by this particular bias as is evidenced by the considerable amount of attention they have devoted to the fear of death and the dead among "primitive" peoples. The point is that this so-called primitive behavior may have been no less loving or sorrowful than our own type of mourning, but this possibility was not even considered by the observers, for such behavior did not conform "with [the ethnographers] well-defined standards of propriety for all the great crises of life."[9]

The cultural shock bias is hardly restricted to the work of ethnographers, and it shows up regularly in death research. Mitford travelled to this country from her home in Britain to study and write about *The American Way of Death.* Being British, it is not surprising that she was quite critical of the American manner of displaying the corpse, the use of cosmetic embalming, and the various other techniques used for attracting attention to the body of the dead,[10] for display of the corpse is stigmatized by most Britains as being reprehensible.

It should be pointed out here that one obviously need not leave his society to experience a cultural shock bias. Particularly in a large heterogeneous society like the United States, the death values, attitudes and customs of another social class, ethnic group, religion, or geographic region may be equally shocking and thus conducive to distorted perceptions and interpretations on the part of the investigator. The dangers inherent in a cultural shock bias are best appreciated when it is recognized that they lend themselves quite readily to what Ernest Nagel has described as appraising value judgments.[11] Appraising value judgments lead to the interpretation of objects, events, or situations as being either "good" or "bad," "desirable" or "undesirable," a practice which is simply not acceptable in sound scientific discourse.

Another type of bias, which we shall call the *professional bias,* arises out of common traits shared by members of a given profession. Rheingold's opinions indicate that psychiatrists, who contribute heavily to research on death attitudes, provide a good example of the professional bias. Psychiatrists share the same death fear and counterphobic tendencies of other physicians.[12] They also have a theoretical orientation, acquired during their training, which sees the fear of death as a derivation of some other process, such as the castration complex; this makes them even less objective in their observations of behavior patterns.[13] As Rheingold has stated, "We then have the anomalous situation of persons with defensive and ideological resistance trying to understand what death means to other persons."[14] It is likely that other professional orientations may similarly reveal traits which interfere with objective observation and interpretation in death research. The problem suggests a potentially fruitful and important area for further investigation.

The *involvement bias* stems from the nature and degree of one's emotional involvement with death. As the way we view death is dependent in large part on our prior experiences with it, if the investigator is too involved with death emotionally, or if his peculiar experiences with death have instilled strong attitudes, his discovery of different types of attitudes and emotions and his behavioral interpretations may not meet the scientific criteria of adequate objectivity. Gorer, for example, includes an autobiographical introduction in his book in which he recounts numerous losses of relatives and friends through death—the death of his brother from cancer, the death of his father when the *Lusitania* sank—the apprehension he experienced on viewing a body for the first time, animal deaths which affected him, and numerous other traumatic experiences associated with death and mourning. One cannot help but think that these many shattering mourning experiences must have played some part in bringing him to the conclusion, based on his research, that the present British mourning customs have such serious social and psychological consequences for the mourners that they should be replaced with new ones.[15]

Yet another bias which interferes with sound death research is what we shall call the *other motivated bias.* In this context, "other motivated" is not taken in its customary sense to mean being concerned with others more than with one's self. Quite to the contrary, it refers to the sad fact that some researchers in this field are evidently *motivated* by forces *other* than the objective pursuit of knowledge. Through its sensational writing style, constant use of humor, argument by innuendo and insinuation, relentless attack on the funeral industry without consideration of some of its possibly redeeming qualities, Mitford's analysis of the funeral industry gives one the impression that she is more interested in selling copy than in contributing valid and reliable knowledge.[16] In a similar vein, Riley's research revealed that 80% of a sample chose the response alternative indicating that they "feel it is best to try to make some plans about death," rather than the other alternative, a uniquely worded choice, "I feel it's best to ignore the subject of death and not try to make any kind of plans for when the time comes." In this particular study Riley also concluded that Americans approach death with a "...note of practical realism..." because a large proportion of the population buys life insurance.[17] It could not possibly have been pure coincidence that at the time he drew this conclusion in his role of social scientist, he also held the title "Vice-President and Director of Social Research, The Equitable Life Assurance Society of the United States."[18]

In addition to the four specific biases considered thus far, one final type, *the normative bias,* is perhaps the most common one to become evident in the acceptance-denial controversy. This bias is fostered by the value judgments made by researchers of death attitudes as to what they feel the American attitude toward death should or ought to be. The normative bias seems so widespread, in fact, that what apparently lures many researchers into the field of death attitudes is not a desire to discover whether Americans hold an attitude of acceptance or denial, but rather to determine what the American attitude toward death is, so that they can assign it an appraising value judgment of either "good" or "bad".[19] Virtually all of the researchers who maintain that the characteristic American attitude is one of acceptance, for example, at least implicitly suggest that the acceptance of death is "good" while its denial is "bad." One gets the distinct impression from reading the research that those Americans who accept death are stable, pragmatic realists, while those tending toward death denial should be reported to the Committee on Un-American Activities. In line with this argument, it seems that whichever side of the acceptance-denial controversy is supported by the investigator, acceptance is considered commendable while denial is, to varying degrees, cast as undesirable. These kinds of value judgments on the merit, rightness, or desirability of various death attitudes may frequently distort research findings in that what the researcher seeks and sees is severely circumscribed by his particular view of society. For example, if he feels that Americans are "bad," and that the attitude of denial is also "bad," he might tend to give more credence to behavior which exhibits denial and to interpret some behavior as reflecting denial when in reality it could be a viable reflection of either attitude.

The five biases which we have considered may seriously hamper the integrity of the unwitting investigator in the direction of his study, the selection of his sample, the development of his research design, his selection of specific techniques, the interpretations of his findings, and his arrival at conclusions.

Deficiencies in questioning techniques

A third major type of methodological problem encountered in research on death attitudes stems from the fact that a variety of data gathering techniques used, ranging from questionnaires and interviews to autobiographical information, all share the assumption that man is capable of verbalizing his attitudes toward death. The question posed here is whether the responses people give to questions about the nature of their attitudes accurately reflect their true feelings. Since questioning techniques constitute the most prevalent media for acquiring information about American death attitudes, the issue of their general validity is a crucial one indeed.

Typifying the assumption that people can verbalize their attitudes on death is a statement by Wendell Swenson found in the conclusion of his report on a study of the death attitudes of the aged. He confidently concluded that

> The first and perhaps most significant result of this investigation is that it has demonstrated that death attitudes can objectively be measured with a structured psychometric device.... It is apparent that to obtain a 'death attitude' from an individual, one need merely ask some direct questions about it.[20]

The appearance of such an unsupported conclusion in scholarly writing is indeed astounding. The investigator did little more than simply ask a group of aged people about their attitudes toward death. As a result, the study neither proved, nor was it designed to prove, that the attitudes obtained were actually those held by the respondents. Nowhere is there to be found indication of the use of any other technique as a validity check on the stated attitudes. Furthermore, while his purpose in studying the aged is ostensibly to discover what their attitude toward death might be, he states that by direct questioning one can "...obtain a death attitude...." The phrasing "*a* death attitude," as opposed to *the* attitude or *the actual* attitude, carries with it the implicit assumption that researchers are interested in obtaining any attitude toward death, regardless of whether or not the subject actually holds that attitude. If such is the case, all the investigator has to do is to write a series of possible death attitudes on slips of paper, place them in a hat, and draw one. Thus, like Swenson, he will obtain "...a death attitude...."

The questions asked by students of death attitudes are highly varied, covering a very wide range of attitudes and experiences. Respondents are typically expected to give accurate and reliable answers to such questions as "Explain why, or why not, you would like to live after death;" "Is your own death probable to you?"; "Are you afraid of dying?"; "Are you afraid of death?"; "Are you afraid of being dead?"; "How did you feel about [death] as a child?"; and "...did disease change your attitude?" While we are not claiming that responses to such questions are necessarily inaccurate or unreliable, there are several reasons why data collected through this type of questioning should not be relied upon too heavily as viable representations of attitudes actually held.

First, many respondents may consider the raising of such questions an invasion of privacy and consequently may be unwilling to give accurate answers. Talcott Parsons, for example, has correctly observed that the privacy of many areas of human life is institutionally protected in this society, with death attitudes being one such protected area, "...a private affair into which others should not casually probe."[21] In general, we do not feel that one should ask questions about what we consider a personal part of our lives, unless the questioner is close to us emotionally. This fact is illustrated in a story told by the late F.W.H. Myers of how he asked a man at a dinner table what he thought would happen to him when he died. The man tried to ignore the question, but on being pressed he replied, "Oh well, I suppose I shall inherit eternal bliss, but I wish you wouldn't talk about such unpleasant subjects."[22]

A second factor to be considered in assessing the general reliability and validity of questioning techniques is that, even if the respondents were willing to provide answers that were as accurate as possible, they might still be unable to give truly viable information. Many of the questions require them to deal with past death experiences and attitudes, the change in their attitudes over time, and the effect of past experiences on their present conceptions. In short, the questions require an ability to remember correctly how one felt or acted at some time in the past and, occasionally, an ability to recognize the causality of changes. Given the generally emotional nature of the events being recalled, the memory requirement seems especially difficult to fulfill. A study by Neilson, for example, reveals that people's memories of experiences in which they were emotionally involved cannot be relied upon.[23] Subjects took part in a discussion about their personal philosophies and values with a "stooge" who had been paid to deliberately antagonize and criticize the naive participants. The subjects were quite unaware that the "stooge" was not just another subject, but were cognizant of the fact that they were being filmed during the discussion and that they would see the film replayed later. At the conclusion of the verbal exchanges, the subjects questioned were only aware that their actions were more vivid during the discussion. This was quite unusual, since

> A good deal of forceful emotion was manifested, although the subjects did not realize this during the discussion and denied it immediately afterwards in a post-dyadic interview.[24]

It was not until they viewed the film that they realized how they had really acted. Some subjects did not become aware of their emotional involvement in the discussion even after they had seen the film; it was not until a second screening, a year and a half after the initial viewing, that they fully realized the extent of their emotional reactions. In light of this evidence, responses about past experiences with death and death attitudes are indeed suspect. This problem is enhanced by the fact that the American view of death is enshrouded by strong emotional involvement and taboos, and that "behavior associated with strong social taboos is frequently repressed."[25]

Even if it could be assumed that respondents earnestly desire to give accurate replies, and further, that they possess the ability to recall their experiences precisely, they may still demonstrate difficulties in giving concise representations of their attitudes because of problems with verbalization. Feelings are generally complex and are therefore not conducive to facile or accurate verbal expression. Attitudes toward death would no doubt rank very high on a scale of verbalization difficulty. *Ceteris paribus,* the more a person reflects upon or discusses his attitudes on a subject, the more exact his description becomes; but the American taboo on death conversation almost precludes the development of a familiarity with the vocabulary and techniques involved in the discussion of death attitudes. In many instances, in fact, a subject's response might represent his very first attempt to verbalize his attitudes toward death. Furthermore, since death is not ordinarily discussed, there is little cause or chance for the genesis of more sophisticated and precise terminology with which to discuss it; the respondent thus has no tools with which to accurately express his attitudes.

The characteristic American pride in rationality may also function to alter the nature of attitudinal responses. One of the distinguishing features of rationality is consistency, and a concern with consistency may give rise to some interesting kinds of biases, particularly as related to such an emotion-laden topic as death. For example, in an effort not to appear inconsistent to the investigator, a subject may indicate that he fears death and never looks forward to it when, in fact, he *does* fear death but still *does* look forward to it. In this situation, a statement of the respondent's true attitudes would make him appear irrational, both to himself and to the researcher; he consequently misrepresents his feelings to maintain an aura of rationality. In general, people are quite inconsistent in their attitudes, a tendency which is not often revealed in their questionnaire responses.

Although not necessarily inherent in the procedures themselves, one final problem relating to the use of questioning techniques is that they frequently force the information desired by the interviewer be it valid for the subject being questioned, or not. This happens in at least two ways: First, some questions are phrased in such a fashion as to predispose the respondent to reply in a certain manner, quite possibly contrary to his actual beliefs. Other types of questions inherently assume that individuals have answers to them when, in fact, they may not. For example, "What have you learned from your recent funeral experience?" assumes that something has been learned, and "What time of day do you usually think about death?" assumes that there is some specific time at which the respondent thinks about death. These types of questions often force the individual to fabricate or modify his reply, or to restructure his perceptions in order to make them fit the question.

Thus there are many good reasons to doubt the wisdom of the current heavy reliance on questioning techniques for acquiring information on death attitudes. The following statement from Milton Rokeach's *Beliefs, Attitudes and Values* is especially applicable to the field of death research, and serves as a fitting conclusion to this section:

> When a person says, 'This I believe,...' he may, or may not, be representing accurately what he truly believes because there are often compelling personal and social reasons, conscious and unconscious, why he will not or cannot tell us... [Beliefs] cannot be directly observed but must be inferred as best one can, with whatever devices are available, from all the things one says and does.[26]

Deficiencies in projective devices

We have seen the pitfalls, in the above discussion, of the characteristic heavy reliance on direct questioning techniques, especially when they constitute the sole means for obtaining attitudinal data; a more responsible and effective strategy is indicated. A seemingly wiser course might be to use more covert psychological projective techniques. Unfortunately, however, it is precisely these apparently "unobtrusive" measuring devices which present us with the fourth major methodological problem of death attitude research.

Ostensibly, projective psychological tests are intended to uncover attitudes which are generally considered to be found in the subconscious, attitudes which are severely repressed and almost inextricably interwoven with one another. The problem is that the question of instrument validity characteristically remains a moot one. A critical examination of three selected projective techniques which have found favor with students of death research should suffice to convey the problematic nature of their implementation.

The *sentence completion test* is designed to uncover certain repressed attitudes by requiring subjects to complete a series of previously prepared partial sentences as rapidly as possible. This test is founded on the assumption that when a person is forced to work at maximum speed he will give the first response which comes to mind, this initial response being representative of his most strongly felt attitudes. The responses thus obtained are then scrutinized for emerging patterns, such as repeated references to death rites, customs, or practices, or to a fear of judgment after death, and so on. Finally, the responses of all the subjects are systematically classified according to these various categories by a panel of three judges.

There are several reasons for doubting the ability of the sentence completion test to yield valid attitudinal data concerning death. For example, many of the partial sentences used by Faunce and Fulton in their study seemed to force a particular type of response. Illustrative are certain items requiring an answer depicting action, the possibility of inaction or rest being precluded by the suggestive phraseology: "When a man dies, he _____;" "The person in the room was dead, so I _____;" and "When I was told I had six weeks to live, I _____."[27] In addition to its tendency to force answers, the sentence completion test may also lend itself quite readily to what may be described as a *momentum effect*, further increasing the likelihood of nonrepresentative responses. Since one is required to work as rapidly as possible, it is highly probable that the same kind of thinking or mental set employed in arriving at the first response will be repeated further along in the test. The subject is precluded from taking the time to think of more accurate and precise ways of expressing his attitudes; the first thing coming to mind might often be more a function of a recently given response than of one's real feelings. The tendency of humans to economize on perception and thinking has been amply demonstrated and needs no elaboration here. In a similar vein, our attitudes toward death are ordinarily complex and possess subtle shades of meaning, thereby rendering single-phrase responses simplistic representations, at best. Further, it should not be forgotten that the data provided by the sentence completion test do not reveal attitudes directly and thus call for an indeterminate amount of interpretation which is perennially problematic. The categorization process is, similarly, an important potential source of error, for the types of categories selected necessarily structure the results of the study to some extent: If the investigator classifies all responses into three general classes, there may develop a strong inclination to conclude that people hold but three kinds of attitudes. Also, in addition to the inevitably subjective classification procedure, responses which may actually exhibit varying magnitudes or intensities of the property under consideration are treated as though they were quantitatively equivalent, regardless of important shades of difference. All in all, therefore, the validity of the sentence completion technique as applied to death research is at best questionable.

The *word association test* has also been employed by students of death research. As it shares the design of the sentence test, in that it is intended to uncover attitudes by seeking rapid responses to verbal cues, it shares many of its defects. One particular use of the word association test differs from that of the sentence completion test, however, and it deserves additional comment.

The word association test is frequently employed to determine the strength of the subjects' emotional reactions to death-associated words. The subject is requested to respond with the first word which comes to mind after hearing each of the cue words, which are of two major types, basal or non-emotive words (such as chair or desk) and death words. The subject's degree of emotional involvement is calculated by comparing the amount of time it takes him to respond to death as opposed to basal stimuli. The rationale behind the test assumes that the longer it takes the subject to respond, the more emotionally involved he is with the topic and the more repressed are his attitudes about it. A second technique, the galvanic skin response test (the G.S.R.) is often added as a check. The G.S.R., commonly called a "lie detector," measures the subject's emotional response to each word through the amount of perspiration resulting from the tension elicited by the cue word. Thus, a subject taking but two seconds to respond to the word "table," might require fifteen in overtly reacting to the stimulus "corpse," and the galvanic reading would concomitantly indicate a low response to "table" and a high one to "corpse." The difference between the reactions to the two cue words is considered to reflect differential degrees of emotional involvement with the topics of which the stimuli are symbolic.

Even when taken in conjunction, it is questionable whether the word association test and the G.S.R. do indeed reveal the degree of repression of death attitudes or of emotional involvement with death. It may very well be that the tension causing the variation in response is a direct result of the American taboo on death conversation, of an "...awareness of the impact of this topic on others."[28] The recorded tension might be due to the subject's concern over how others will react to his particular feelings about death. Thus, the ostensible evidence may be a function of "cultural influence" rather than of emotional involvement with death.[29] The taboo on death conversation may further disturb test results in that it allows neither for the growth of a death-related vocabulary nor for meaningful responses and response patterns. Consequently, the longer time required for reacting to death-associated words may be merely an indication of the difficult search for an appropriate term, rather than of repression.

Finally, it is eminently reasonable to suggest that the word association and galvanic skin response tests do not provide viable checks for one another as intended, for they seem to set in motion what may aptly be called a *vicious circle*. The presumptive vicious circle begins when a subject cannot respond quickly to a death word. His failure is disconcerting, his tension level climbs, and the galvanic reading jumps. The increased tension makes it still more difficult to conjure up an appropriate response, the awareness of flying time pushes the tension level still higher, up further goes the G.S.R., and so on. In short, it is quite conceivable that the word association test and the G.S.R. are measuring tension generated by a variety of factors other than death-related attitudes and repressions. In all probability, these tests may in actuality be reflecting a combination of extraneous factors and death attitudes simultaneously. What is most important in this regard is that one cannot be even reasonably certain that the test measures what it is purported to measure.

The final covert psychological projective technique to be considered here is the *Thematic Apperception Test*. This test is particularly interesting: For once test subjects, who are often studied by researchers with devices designed to conceal the true purpose of the study, get the last laugh at researchers who have unwittingly deceived themselves with their own techniques. The Thematic Apperception Test (commonly referred to as the T.A.T.) has been used by death researchers to investigate the nature of death attitudes and the degree of the subjects' concern with death. The subject is presented with a picture which is ostensibly *not* related to death and he is asked to tell a story about it. His concern about death is disclosed by the frequency with which death appears in the manufactured stories, while the nature of his attitudes is revealed through an examination of the content of the death references. There are numerous problems as to the validity and reliability of the T.A.T., most notably those deriving from the highly subjective interpretations of the death references in the stories. A recent finding by Rhudick and Dibner suggests that the T.A.T.'s use in the past may not have revealed concern over death at all.[30] In the course of their own study, these investigators found that certain pictures elicited death themes far more frequently than others. What this finding implies, of course, is that when the researchers chose pictures which they thought to be free of death connotations, they were unconsciously motivated to choose those which would prompt death responses. When a subject responded to these pictures with death themes, it was naively concluded that he possessed a high degree of concern about death; in actuality, such a response might easily have been more a function of the picture than of the peculiarities of the subject. Once again we discover a test of dubious credibility.

The implementation of each of the three projective tests discussed above is problematic since their validity is highly debatable. We conclude this section with one final observation which further calls their effectiveness into question: It will be recalled that these techniques are primarily designed to uncover attitudes which are subconscious and highly repressed. Presumably these attitudes are so repressed because the subject feels a need, most generally due to one or more of the emotional forces discussed earlier, to repress them.[31] Merely asking a subject to complete a sentence or to tell a story does not eliminate his strongly felt need to repress his true feelings. Depending upon the strength of such a need, it is probable that repressed attitudes will remain inaccessible, even in the face of highly suggestive or provocative stimuli.

Over-interpretation of data

A fifth problem contributing to the contradictory findings in the area of death research, and thereby providing further impetus to the acceptance-denial controversy, is the tendency of investigators to overinterpret the data which they collect. Leon Saul's analysis of the behavior of a doctor who discovers that he has terminal cancer provides an instance of such over-interpretation.[32] Saul first notes that, "He [the doctor] made arrangements, for example, to turn in his automobile for a model he preferred, and he made other plans that would be rational only if he were to live for a long time."[33] Saul interprets this behavior as irrational, evidently assuming that any purchase which is not economically advantageous is necessarily irrational. He neglects the obvious possibility that the doctor may have quite rationally decided that since he had only a short time to live, he should enjoy a few luxuries before his life ends. The doctor reportedly also took a drug which he knew would probably not be of any help in averting his impending death, an action once again interpreted by Saul as an indication of reality denial: "Now he said that he knew of course that it was probably valueless, but since nothing was to be lost he would try it."[34] This reaction is hardly, as Saul termed it, "delusional." Although the doctor did indeed seem to recognize that the drug probably would not work, extreme situations characteristically call for extreme, "last ditch" efforts. In fact, there is no good reason to suppose that the doctor would not have given the same drug to one of his patients under similar circumstances. Finally, Saul observes that "Regressive elements were clear in his attitude toward his wife whom he called 'mother' and whom he wished to hold his hand at the end."[35] Are we to accept the portrayal of this behavior as "regressive?" In later years, husbands and wives often refer to each other as "mother" and "father," a habit acquired while their children were growing up. Also, in their relationships with their husbands, wives are usually part mothers, and the doctor was probably only verbalizing this fact. Finally, one finds it most difficult to agree with Saul that the dying man's desire to have his wife take his hand at the end is indicative of regressive tendencies. Taking the hand of one's wife at the time of death would seem most natural.

With a significant number of researchers making interpretations of the kind described above, it is almost amazing that more contradiction does not exist in the field. Every effort must be made to guard against over-interpretation, for while those who are not social scientists may interpret data as common sense dictates, we must be more cautious and skeptical. As one minister has put it,

> We are accustomed to such stretching of the data [beyond the actual findings] in the ministerial meditations on dying; data-free interpretation is a priestly prerogative. But over interpretation may be as common among psychoanalysts and journalists for whom the death scene has become 'big.' [36]

Problems of conceptualization

The sixth and final major methodological problem fostering the characteristic inconsistencies and conflicts in death research findings is a function of unclear, inexplicit conceptualization. Symptomatic of this difficulty is the fact that prior to embarking upon a particular research endeavor, many investigators frequently do not have a clearly defined, defensible, exact conception of what it is they are seeking. While they may well have singled out one or more concepts of interest, these are most often intuitively derived and lacking in clear empirical referents.[37] In light of the pervasive presence of these "isolated abstract concepts," one can hardly ever be sure of what it is that particular behavior patterns can validly be said to exhibit,[38] nor are we easily able to decide upon viable criteria for determining the correct interpretations of behaviors.

In Chapter Two, for example, we argued that numerous research findings may be seriously misleading because the meanings of such concepts as "fear of death" and "attitudes toward death" are not nearly explicit enough. Similarly, we further indicated the need to distinguish between "being dead" and "dying." The failure to make such crucial distinctions may lead to distorted and even meaningless results. For example, many of the studies claiming to have revealed the presence of the fear of death to a marked degree may actually have promoted gross inaccuracies, due to the failure to distinguish clearly between the "fear of death" and the "fear of the process of dying." It is highly probable that the investigators were measuring both fears to some undetermined and unspecified extent.

Still more problematic in the present context are the vague conceptualization and the concomitant contradictions in usage of the concepts 'acceptance' and 'denial'; while these may be concepts adequate for a general discussion of attitudes, there is good reason to believe that they are not entirely suitable for research purposes. This indeterminacy becomes clearer when it is recognized that the concepts are evidently so loosely formulated that the same phenomenon can often be used as an example of *either acceptance or denial* of death. Depending upon the investigator, identical behavioral patterns may be classed in diametrically opposite ways. For example, on the one hand euphemisms for death are said to reflect a denial attitude, since the word "death" is avoided and its reality thus hidden or masked. On the other hand, however, the same euphemisms are held to reflect attitudinal acceptance in that they are often graphic descriptions of the crasser aspects of death, and therefore call attention to, rather than mask, death. Consider also the researchers' interpretations of our period of mourning, which is short as compared to that of many other cultures: Whereas proponents of the death denial argument are prone to, contend that the short period of mourning is indicative of denial since it allows us to rid ourselves of the reminders of death as soon as possible, advocates of the opposing position interpret the brief mourning period as acceptance, for the grief work is done quickly, death is readily accepted, and people easily return to their normal routines.

The fact that the same phenomenon may be considered evidence of both acceptance and denial forcefully suggests that neither concept is formulated clearly enough for research purposes and that the distinction between what each attitude entails has not been adequately specified. Deficiencies in conceptualization are obviously not unique to death research, for they are similar to those plaguing the conceptual domain of sociology as a whole. Most sociological concepts, particularly those of the phenomenological variety, are not embedded within the propositional networks of well-supported "explicit theories," and they are consequently lacking in "epistemic significance."[39] That is to say they lack demonstrable connections,

> ...either directly or indirectly, to observables by rules of correspondence that have been empirically justified; i.e., via these rules, confirmed relationships have been established between observable concepts and theoretical concepts.[40]

In view of the substantial methodological problems presented in this chapter it becomes clearer why research on death attitudes has yielded such contradictory findings. Upon examining contemporary writings on death attitudes, one finds himself "...|swimming| in a sea of *non sequitur* unsupported assertion, and conflicting readings of meanings."[41] Having surveyed the major problems of general methodological shoddiness, investigator bias, deficiencies in questioning techniques and projective devices, over-interpretation of data, and problems of conceptualization, one must indeed be surprised that there exists as much agreement as there does in the field.

These problems are not necessarily insurmountable as regards future research, however. Our discussion indicates a most pressing need for more responsible research; for a constructive awareness on the part of investigators of their individual biases; for marked improvement in existing techniques; for more skeptical and cautious interpretation of data; for more carefully formulated and explicated concepts; and for research implementing a combination of a wide variety of techniques which would provide a relia-ble series of crosschecks, as well as allow the discernment of attitudes operating on both the conscious and subconscious levels of awareness. Hopefully, we have arrived at a satisfactory partial explanation for the inconsistent and contradictory findings which have prompted the ac-ceptance-denial controversy. In the following chapters we advance ad-ditional reasons for these disagreements, and we suggest a partial resolu-tion of the controversy.

NOTES

1. I. E. Alexander and A. M. Alderstein, "Affective Responses to the Concept of Death in a Population of Children and Early Adolescents," *Journal of Genetic Psychology,* 1958, 93, p. 169.
2. *Ibid.,* p. 169.
3. M.H. Nagy, "The Child's View of Death," in Herman Feifel (ed.), *The Meaning of Death,* New York: McGraw-Hill Book Company, Inc., 1959, pp. 79-98.
4. G. Murphy, "Discussion," in *ibid.,* pp. 321-322.
5. H. Becker, "The Sorrow of Bereavement," *Journal of Abnormal and Social Psychology,* 1933, 27, pp. 391-410.
6. R. Fulton, "The Sacred and the Secular: Attitudes of the American Public toward Death, Funerals, and Funeral Directors," in Robert Fulton (ed.), *Death and Identity,* New York: John Wiley and Sons, Inc., 1965, pp. 89-105.
7. *Ibid.,* p. 90.
8. A. Kaplan, *The Conduct of Inquiry: Methodology for Behavioral Science,* San Francisco: Chandler Publishing Company, 1964, p. 373.
9. Becker, *op. cit.,* p. 391.
10. J. Mitford, *The American Way of Death,* New York: Simon and Schuster, 1963.
11. Ernest Nagel, *The Structure of Science: Problems in the Logic of Scientific Explanation,* New York: Harcourt, Brace & World, Inc., 1961, pp. 492-495.
12. J.C. Rheingold, *The Mother, Anxiety and Death,* Boston: Little, Brown and Company, 1967, p. 34.
13. *Ibid.,* p. 34.
14. *Ibid.,* p. 34.
15. Gorer summarized in C. Driver, "The Great Unmentionable," *Atlas,* August, 1965, 10, p. 113.
16. Mitford, *op. cit.*

17. J.W. Riley, Jr., "Contemporary Society and the Institution of Life Insurance," *Journal of the American Society of Chartered Life Underwriters,* 1964, 18, pp. 102-103.
18. *Ibid.,* p. 93.
19. See Nagel, *op. cit.,* pp. 492-495.
20. W.M. Swenson, "Attitudes toward Death Among the Aged," in Fulton, *op. cit.,* pp. 109-110.
21. T. Parsons, "Death in American Society: A Brief Working Paper," *American Behavioral Scientist,* 1963, 6, p. 63.
22. Cited in B. Russell, "Your Child and the Fear of Death," *The Forum,* 1929, 81, p. 175.
23. G.S. Neilson, "The Method of Self Confrontation," in Robert White (ed.), *The Study of Lives,* New York: Atherton Press, 1963, pp. 125-141.
24. *Ibid.,* p. 126.
25. G. Lehner and E. Kube, *The Dynamics of Personal Adjustment,* Englewood Cliffs, N.J.: Prentice-Hall, Inc., 1964, p. 138.
26. M. Rokeach, *Beliefs, Attitudes and Values,* San Francisco: Jossey-Bass, Inc., 1968, p. 2.
27. W.A. Faunce and R.L. Fulton, "The Sociology of Death: A Neglected Area of Research," *Social Forces,* 1958, 36, p. 207.
28. Alexander and Alderstein, *op. cit.,* p. 174.
29. *Ibid.,* p. 174.
30. P.J. Rhudick and A.S. Dibner, "Age, Personality, and Health Correlates of Death Concerns in Normal Aged Individuals," *Journal of Gerontology,* 1961, 16, pp. 44-49.
31. See Chapter Two on the fear of death and the death wish.
32. L.J. Saul, "Reactions of a Man to Natural Death," *Psychoanalytic Quarterly,* 1959, 28, pp. 383-386.
33. *Ibid.,* p. 384.
34. *Ibid.,* pp. 384-385.
35. *Ibid.,* p. 386.
36. G. Nettler, "Review Essay: On Death and Dying," *Social Problems,* 1967, 14, p. 336.
37. For a discussion concerning problems of concept formation in sociology, see R.G. Dumont and W.J. Wilson, "Aspects of Concept Formation, Explication, and Theory Construction in Sociology," *American Sociological Review,* 1967, 32, pp. 985-995; and W.J. Wilson and R.G. Dumont, "Rules of Correspondence and Sociological Concepts," *Sociology and Social Research,* 1968, 52, pp. 217-227.
38. Dumont and Wilson, *op. cit.*
39. *Ibid.,* p. 987.
40. *Ibid.,* p. 987.
41. Nettler, *op. cit.,* p. 336.

Chapter Six

Individual Variability
of Death Attitudes

*Death is terrible to Cicero,
desirable to Cato, and indifferent to Socrates.*

Traditional Proverb

While the methodological problems discussed in the preceding chapter
have unquestionably played a most important role in prompting the
inconsistencies, ambiguities, and contradictions which have given rise
to the acceptance-denial controversy, the explanation which they offer
is only partial, and the resolution of the controversy continues to await
explicit formulation. The intent of the present chapter is to attempt to
further pursue the explanation and to move closer to a successful resolution by demonstrating a flaw in one of the fundamental assumptions
underlying the acceptance-denial controversy. Specifically, available
evidence strongly suggests that it is quite untenable to assume that there
exists *an* "American" attitude toward death.

Before proceeding, the reader should be cautioned that a number of
studies cited in this monograph suffer to some extent from one or more
of the deficiencies which have been reviewed in the preceding chapter.
This is of course inevitable, and the difficulties thereby entailed are readily conceded. In the absence of more definitive and "puristic" studies,
however, selective reference has been made primarily to those studies
which exhibit the highest available levels of validity, reliability, and
general sophistication. Furthermore, in this and the following chapter,
the intended focus is upon those studies which are mutually supportive
in their theoretical implications, as well as being largely consistent with
the matrix of accumulated social scientific knowledge.

To reiterate, a key supposition underlying the acceptance-denial controversy is that there exists a single and uniquely "American" attitude
toward death. This attitude, be it acceptance or denial, is not typically
thought to be "American" solely because the majority of American people
hold it, but rather because it is believed to be held by the "society,"
imbedded in and imparted by the American culture. This unwarranted
assumption probably has its historical antecedents in the contributions

of anthropologists and ethnographers who studied the death customs and attitudes of preliterates, long before American attitudes were investigated. These pioneering scholars of death discovered attitudes and practices which were virtually uniform throughout the culture, attitudes which were homogeneous products of a homogeneous culture, transmitted to every member by the society. For example, there was quite clearly an Ulithi attitude toward death, held by all members of that society, which was notably distinct from that of the Ibo society. Thus, in these and in similar situations, death attitudes were truly societal and cultural products. With such precedents, it would seem natural to assume the existence of an "American" attitude, the concomitant research task being solely to discover its peculiar nature. The culture and society of the United States are not homogeneous entities as were their primitive counterparts, however, and it has become increasingly difficult to find an uniquely "American" attitude toward anything.

Unwarranted generalizations have too often been explicitly or implicitly advanced by unwitting investigators who, upon testing a group of American subjects and finding the preponderance of a particular attitude, have naively assumed the revealed attitude to be representatively American: one researcher will study a group, discover that the majority of his subjects accept death, and then conclude that the "American" attitude toward death is one of acceptance; while a second researcher will test a second group, find that his subjects tend to deny death, and then claim an "American" attitude of death denial. We suggest that such glaringly discrepant findings may be due largely to the fact that it has been incorrectly assumed that the attitude characterizing the group has its genesis in the society or culture, rather than being a coincidental product of those particular individuals constituting the group. Different groups of individuals have been tested, each having unique backgrounds, varied personal experiences with death, various expectations from life, and, as a result, dissimilar *individual* attitudes toward death.

Preliminary support for our contention of attitudinal individuation is provided by recalling our discussion of death attitude formation in Chapter One, where it was discovered that the individual in the United States is generally left to his own devices in the development of his attitudes toward death by his parents, by the general culture, and by those institutions which have important socialization functions in other crucial areas of human experience.[1] Furthermore, as Parsons has indicated, in the United States a person's thoughts, beliefs, and attitudes toward death are considered to be personal and private matters.[2] In light of the fact that American attitudes toward death are formulated in a process marked by personal development or maturation, rather than through cultural transmission, it is logical to expect significant variability in the resultant death attitudes. Available research evidence lends support to our argument, for a sufficient number of relevant variables have been isolated to indicate that death attitudes are indeed subject to marked individual variability. Sex, religion, and age are three of the more important of those factors affecting death attitudes.

In Chapter Two we observed that women generally reveal a stronger death wish than do men. Empirical research also demonstrates that females seem to think about death more frequently and that they respond to it with greater fear.[3] This variation in views and emotional responses points to a fundamental difference in the significance which men and women attach to death. The American female learns quite early in life that it is her role to please those close to her, and that the successful fulfillment of this function will earn her the love which she has come to need. As a consequence, she is more likely to feel that love is lost at the time of death, since it signals the termination of her capacity to please.[4] Furthermore, death apparently has a greater number of physical associations for the female. Although the precise reasons for this phenomenon remain indeterminate, it seems to derive primarily from the fact that a woman's physical beauty, a main factor in her ability to please in this society, is lost both through the approach to death (old age) as well as through death itself. In fact, a woman's physical associations with death are so salient and strong that her death fears are more pronounced during sexual maturation, menstruation, childbirth, and menopause than at any other time.[5] Women also have a tendency to be more overt in their attitudes toward death, and they appear less reticent to reveal them to others.[6]

While men and women have been found to differ little in their beliefs and practices as regards most death-related social issues, such as birth control, euthanasia, and the like, men have been observed to accept wartime killing in significantly greater proportions than women.[7] Additional sex-related variations seem to be indicated by differential responses to the Thematic Apperception Test, with women developing stories having as their dominant theme the loss of the deceased, and as a secondary theme, women dying and being mourned. On this same test men revealed a dominant theme of violence and mutilation, with secondary themes depicting death as frustration and failure.[8] Finally, variation in male and female attitudes toward death is found in the results of a preliminary study which showed women to be more favorably disposed toward traditional religious views on death and toward the presence of the family at the time of death, as well as "More disturbed by Ugly Death and Fear of Burial; [while] men indicate[d] a significantly greater enjoyment of life and a higher score on Destructive Impulsivity."[9]

Although more information is available concerning the question of the relationship between religion and death attitudes, it generally appears less conclusive than the evidence on sex-related variations. As our discussion of Chapter Two indicated, the nature and direction of the relations obtaining between religion and our emotional responses to death, namely the fear of death and the death wish, are unresolved and extremely problematical. Research conducted on the relationship between religion and death attitudes reveals this same indeterminacy, and it does so for basically the same reasons. As Martin and Wrightsman have observed, investigations employing the religious variable have been deficient in a number of important respects: insufficient attention has been paid to the likely differences among the religious groups; the use of quantitative data and statistical analysis has been typically overlooked; the extent of the subjects' death contacts has been ignored; and various other sound methodological techniques and refinements have been either conspicuously absent or misused.[10] Consequently, resultant findings and conclusions have exhibited little explanatory or predictive import.

Valid insights into this vital problem area are rendered yet more elusive in light of the major and fundamental changes occurring in American religions today, changes which nearly preclude the discernment of unambiguous causal linkages. A recent study of popular religion in the United States suggests, however, that the changes which are occurring are likely to have significant consequences for death attitudes. In particular, there appears to be a notable shift in emphasis under way from a belief in salvation in an afterlife to a belief in salvation in this life, and a concomitant decrease in attention to inspirational writings concerned with spiritual preparation for death, almost to the point of neglect.[11] Within Protestant religions in particular, the organized religious response to death is becoming increasingly secular, with the clergy feeling more and more that its primary function at funerals is to give aid and comfort to the living, rather than to attend to the needs of the dead.[12]

Even if we grant the problematical implications of the changing context of religion and religious belief and practice in the United States, some support can yet be advanced to indicate that the religious variable does indeed affect individual death attitudes. For example, although both religious and nonreligious persons exhibit strong emotional involvement with death and assign "bad" and "potent" values to death words, the more religious apparently view their deaths more positively and have a greater associated tendency of looking forward to it.[13] This tendency toward death acceptance is particularly characteristic of the more fundamentalist religious groups, where the stalwart belief in the evil doings of Satan functions to reduce or eliminate guilt feelings, thereby making heaven a personally viewed certainty.[14] Further research has also shown that fundamentalist believers and religiously actives reveal very positive death attitudes, while those with little religious activity or interest tend to evade death.[15] Among non-fundamentalist religious persons hell is seemingly viewed as a more real likelihood, and, "possibly because they fear punishment after death, believers see mortality as less positive than do nonbelievers and doubters."[16] In short, it seems that while traditional, fundamentalist types of belief have been associated with death acceptance, "temporal mindedness and scientific skepticism" are coterminous with "death suppression," which leads to attitudes of denial.[17] Furthermore, it is likely that Christianity has a contradictory effect on its adherents, since it offers both a heaven and a hell. Whereas the possibility of the former may render death more acceptable, the simultaneous existence of the latter may lend itself to attitudes of denial. Regardless of the specific attitude or attitudes held, however, most religious Americans probably tend to both fear and dread death, since Christianity

> ...has as a whole used its vast influence to make men dread death. The Buddha's attitude was very different; after his enlightenment experience he transcended all anxiety and the stories of his death represent an outright antithesis to the stories of Christ's dreadful death.[18]

Perhaps the strongest support for the relevancy of the religious variable is provided by Kalish's study which revealed that the denomination or major religious group one belonged to had an amazingly marked and consistent effect on attitudes toward death-related social issues and practices.[19] Roman Catholics, for example, were the most tenaciously in favor of funerals, capital punishment, wartime killing, and traditional religion ("after-life and personal God"). Protestants were less in favor of these concerns, Jews still less, and "atheists/agnostics" least. With respect to the issues of birth control, suicide, euthanasia, and "humanism," the order of acceptance was completely and perfectly reversed, with "atheists/ agnostics" being the strongest proponents and Roman Catholics registering the greatest opposition.[20]

It should come as no surprise to discover that the variable of age seems to play an important role in the determination of death attitudes, particularly in youth, when attitudes develop, and among the aged, when death is at hand. In Chapter One we observed that the child's attitudes toward death tend to become more stable as he grows older, and that they are relatively fixed and sophisticated (though not necessarily organized) by the time he reaches adolescence. There exists a paucity of research on attitude change in adult life as a function of aging, since the bulk of inquiry has focused on adult attitude change resulting from traumatic death experiences.

The effect of age on attitudes toward death-related social issues and beliefs has been found to be virtually negligible, and age apparently bears no relation to the methods individuals employ for coping with the awareness of death.[21] Research into the death attitudes of the elderly, however, clearly reveals age to be a significant variable. For example, an interesting by-product of a study seeking to determine the relevancy of the religious factor was the discovery that, "...contrary to expectation, there is a slight tendency for older members of the congregations to report less fear of death."[22] Independently, Nettler concurs with this finding, pointing out that the aged not only fear death less, but also exhibit a tendency toward looking forward to death when they are in poor health.[23] This evidence would seem to be consistent with the hypothesis of Diggory and Rothman that the death fear stems in large part from the fact that death is viewed as precluding the fulfillment of valued goals.[24] Presumably, by the time one reaches old age he has fulfilled his goals to his satisfaction or, if he has not attained them, has either made them more modest or somehow rationalized his lack of achievement.

While old age ostensibly brings about a decreased fear of death, the response to death by the aged does not necessarily become more positive or adaptive. In fact, concern about death on the part of the elderly is ordinarily accompanied by depression,[25] a natural reaction for many reasons. Primarily because they are no longer defined as "economically useful," because they have become literally marginal members of the society, and because they are frequently forced to live out their last days in the isolation of an old age home, elderly citizens of the United States have a tendency to feel that their deaths will have very little effect upon those who survive them. The death of the elderly person, who is often perceived by himself and others as not needed and troublesome, may even come to be viewed as a welcomed relief from a financial burden.[26] Although the aged person becomes readily depressed when thinking about his own death, by the time he actually dies he has generally made some sort of peace with death and, as a result, it is relatively rare for him to struggle with it.[27]

Related to the variable of age, and yet notably distinct from it, is what we shall label the *subjective time factor*. Tillich contends that one gains cognizance of the existence of time when he becomes aware of the fact that he must die:

> Time runs from the beginning to the end, but our awareness of time goes in the opposite direction. It starts with anxious anticipation of the end. In the light of the future we see the past and present.[28]

While our anticipation of death affects our awareness of time, it also seems reasonable to suppose that the manner in which we perceive time might have consequences for our attitudes toward death. More specifically, if one feels that time is moving quickly, his tendency will be to see death as rapidly approaching, and his proclivity to either accept or deny death might be considerably different from that of a person who is similar in all other relevant respects but who views time as moving very slowly, thereby placing death in the distant future. True, one's exact age may have a significant bearing upon how near he feels to death, since he can easily compare his age to the current average life expectancy to get an approximate fix on the time of death. However, the "subjective" nature of the time factor becomes more obvious when we consider that two men can both be forty years old and, to one death at age seventy appears close at hand, while to the other death at seventy seems in the very distant future. It is quite likely that this subjective time factor is complicated or affected by such variables as one's physical condition, his general level of health, the amount of danger which characterizes his occupation or life style, and his concept of the role of fate, to cite but a few.

While there has apparently been no research dealing specifically with the subjective time factor or with its relationship to death attitudes, indirect support for its significance may be gleaned from various sources, pending more directed and more rigorous evidence. Not surprisingly, studies of combat troops during World War II and also during the Korean Conflict found that men's attitudes toward death are sometimes different after the war is over than they were during the heat of battle. The degree of change is largely due to the change in "the degree of nearness or the degree of displacement from ourselves in terms of time and space..." of death.[29] In terms of our conceptualization, what is even more important is the extent to which one "subjectively" perceives himself as being close to his own death. Two soldiers in battle may be fighting under identical conditions, yet one may feel that he will be hit at any instant while the other is convinced of his invincibility; the former feels death to be "more present" than the latter. In a sense we all experience death long before we die, because "...even before its actual arrival, it is an absent presence."[30] Doubtless, there are numerous events and situations throughout life, such as attending a funeral or having a close brush with death in an auto accident, which make the absent death seem more of a presence.

Further indirect support for the relevancy of the subjective time factor comes from the field of art, in which it has been suggested that our views of time and death are intimately intertwined. For example, Gottlieb reports that one of the symbols most frequently employed by painters to depict death has traditionally been the hourglass. While many of the early symbols have fallen into disuse, the time motif persists in modern paintings: The symbol has changed, however, from the hourglass to the clock and watch, often without hands, with time arrested, and placed in a barren setting, or crawling with insects.[31]

Finally, while he does not do so explicitly, Rheingold suggests the significance of the subjective time factor for death attitudes when he states:

> Attitudes are affected by the time interval the person conceives to exist between the present moment and the moment of death. The age of the person does not necessarily carry implication to him of nearness or remoteness of the end, for some children live with the fear of imminent destruction and some of the aged believe that death will be postponed indefinitely.[32]

In addition to sex, age, religion, and the subjective time factor, other variables have been isolated and shown to affect attitudes toward death. Although they are too numerous to discuss in detail, they include race, degree of concern over one's health, various personality characteristics, social class, living conditions, and educational level.[33] Still other possible relevant variables which merit detailed empirical investigation are the amount of contact with death (quantity of experience), traumatic experiences with death (quality of experience), parental attitudes toward death, emotional security, and the actual condition of one's health. In sum, it can be seen that death attitudes are subject to a marked degree of variation, resulting from the almost innumerable variables which determine and comprise them. Rather than being the unique consequence of a coherent and universal cultural transmission of *an* "American" death attitude, as is explicitly or implicitly assumed by disputants in the acceptance-denial controversy, "attitudes toward death are the result of many interweaving factors..."[34]

In light of the preceding evidence, it would appear that the assumption which underlies the acceptance-denial controversy and its supporting field research is indeed unwarranted. Even Herman Feifel, who continually operates implicitly under this assumption, admits that "...the research in progress reinforces the thinking that death can mean different things to different people."[35] In reviewing twentieth century literature, Hoffman found that, unlike any other epochs in which conceptions of death are uniform for virtually all writers of the period, views on death are now extremely individualistic, reflecting the authors' personal outlooks.[36] Of course, the fact that nearly all authors of any period exhibit similar conceptions also provides strong indication of effective cultural transmission in the molding of attitudes. Gottlieb, as a result of her survey of modern art, contends that contemporary artists will each, "... meet it [death] according to his natural disposition," and that the artist's image of death will usually depend upon his state of mind.[37]

Interested scholars have too long assumed, as did Karl Mannheim, that the individual, "...thinks in the manner in which his group thinks."[38] While this general and valuable sociological directive may be appropriate for inquiry into most areas of human life, it apparently does not apply in the same way to attitudes toward death, at least in contemporary United States society. Because of a proclivity gained through membership in their profession, sociologists have tended to assume that the society has much power over individual attitudes, since these attitudes are believed to be culturally transmitted; this aspect of the sociological imagination needs to be tempered considerably when applied to death attitudes. We do not wish to be misunderstood as claiming that the American *culture* does not embody attitudes toward or beliefs about death, for, as is evidenced by the existence of laws governing murder, suicide, birth control, and disposal of the dead, as well as the somewhat uniform funeral practices and mourning customs, it most certainly does. It is one thing to say that a culture embodies attitudes and beliefs, however, and quite another matter to claim the effective cultural transmission of a meaningful and coherent attitudinal and belief system to the individuals who comprise the society and to the society as a whole. Furthermore, while the culture of the United States exhibits embodiments of various attitudes, it clearly does not embrace *an* "American" attitude toward death.

NOTES

1. L. Bowman, *The American Funeral: A Study in Guilt, Extravagence, and Sublimity*, Washington, D. C.: Public Affairs Press, 1959.
2. T. Parsons, "Death in American Society: A Brief Working Paper," *American Behavioral Scientist*, 1963, 6, p. 63.
3. J. C. Rheingold, *The Mother, Anxiety and Death*, Boston: Little, Brown and Company, 1967, p. 141.
4. M. Chadwick, "Notes Upon the Fear of Death," *International Journal of Psychoanalysis*, 1929, 10, p. 321.
5. *Ibid.*, p. 321; and Rheingold, *op. cit.*, p. 42.
6. *Ibid.*, p. 46.
7. R. A. Kalish, "Some Variables in Death Attitudes," *Journal of Social Psychology*, 1963, 59, p. 144.
8. R. J. Lowry, "Male-Female Differences in Attitudes Toward Death," *Dissertation Abstracts*, 1965, XXVIII, pp. 1607b-1608b.
9. R. A. Kalish, "An Approach to the Study of Death Attitudes," *American Behavioral Scientist*, 1963, 6, p. 69.
10. D. Martin and L. S. Wrightsman, Jr., "The Relationship Between Religious Behavior and Concern About Death," *Journal of Social Psychology*, 1965, 65, pp. 317-318.
11. Schneider and Dornbusch, summarized in M. Rokeach, *Beliefs, Attitudes, and Values*, San Francisco: Jossey-Bass, Inc., 1968.
12. R. L. Fulton, "The Clergyman and The Funeral Director: A Study in Role Conflict," *Social Forces*, 1961, 39, pp. 317-323.

13. See I. E. Alexander and A. M. Alderstein, "Death and Religion," in Herman Feifel (ed.), *The Meaning of Death*, New York: McGraw-Hill Book Company, Inc., 1959, pp. 273-274; and W. M. Swenson, "Attitudes toward Death Among the Aged," in Fulton, *Death and Identity, op. cit.*, p. 110.

14. F. J. Hoffman, "Mortality and Modern Literature," in Feifel, *op. cit.*, p. 135.

15. Swenson, *op. cit.*, pp. 108-109.

16. S. A. Alleman, "The Structure and Content of Belief Systems," *Dissertation Abstracts*, 1964, XXIV, p. 5536b.

17. Rheingold, *op. cit.*, p. 26.

18. W. Kaufmann, "Existentialism and Death," in Feifel, *op. cit.*, pp. 39-63.

19. Kalish, "Some Variables in Death Attitudes," *op. cit.*, pp. 137-145.

20. *Ibid.*, pp. 137-145.

21. See Kalish, "An Approach to the Study of Death Attitudes," *op. cit.*, p. 69; and L. G. Corey, "An Analogue of Resistance to Death Awareness," *Journal of Gerontology*, 1961, 16, pp. 59-60.

22. Martin and Wrightsman, *op. cit.*, p. 323.

23. G. Nettler, "Review Essay: On Death and Dying," *Social Problems*, 1967, 14, p. 341.

24. J. C. Diggory and D. Z. Rothman, "Values Destroyed by Death," *Journal of Abnormal and Social Psychology*, 1961, 63, pp. 205-210.

25. P. J. Rhudick and A. S. Dibner, "Age, Personality, and Health Correlates of Death Concerns in Normal Aged Individuals," *Journal of Gerontology*, 1961, 16, p. 47.

26. Interestingly, a study has been conducted which reveals, contrary to the formulated hypothesis, that depression in the aged *does not* bring about an earlier death. See B. B. Myler, "Depression and Death in the Aged," *Dissertation Abstracts*, 1967, XXVIII, p. 2146.

27. E. Geiringer, "Fear of Death," *Spectator*, August 8, 1952, 189, pp. 179-180.

28. P. Tillich, "The Eternal Now," in Feifel, *op. cit.*, p. 31.

29. G. Murphy, "Discussion," in *ibid.*, p. 336.

30. H. Feifel, "The Taboo on Death," *American Behavioral Scientist*, 1963, 6, p. 66.

31. C. Gottlieb, "Modern Art and Death," in Feifel, *The Meaning of Death, op. cit.*, p. 160.

32. Rheingold, *op. cit.*, pp. 34-35.

33. See Kalish, "An Approach to the Study of Death Attitudes," *op. cit.*, pp. 69-70 on race; Rhudick and Dibner, *op. cit.*, pp. 46-47 on concern over one's health and personality characteristics; W. M. Kephart, "Status After Death," *American Sociological Review*, 1950, 15, pp. 635-643 on social class; and Swenson, *op. cit.*, p. 109 on living conditions and educational level.

31. H. Feifel, "Death," *The Encyclopedia of Mental Health*, 1963, Vol. 2, p. 429.

35. Feifel, "The Taboo on Death," *op. cit.*, p. 67.

36. Hoffman, *op. cit.*

37. Gottlieb, *op. cit.*, p. 167.

38. K. Mannheim, *Ideology and Utopia*, New York: Harcourt, Brace and World, Inc., 1936, p. 3.

Chapter Seven

The Acceptance
Denial Hypothesis

*I have been impressed... with the cultural
contradictions that lie even in deepest scientific thinking about the whole matter [death].*

Gardner Murphy

Although the partial explanations and implicit resolutions contained
within the two preceding chapters may have contributed significantly to
an understanding and appreciation of those factors which have stimulated
the acceptance-denial controversy, one final suggestion is deemed necessary for a full explanation of the contradictory findings and a true resolution of the problem. Specifically, it is the major premise of this chapter
that the controversy has arisen out of a misformulation of the question,
a misformulation which has at once functioned to preclude a successful
resolution. In particular, the characteristic query, "Do Americans accept
or deny their own deaths?", sets up a false dichotomy of mutually
exclusive attitudinal alternatives, for there is substantial evidence to
indicate that the culture of the United States and the individuals in this
society *both* accept *and* deny death, simultaneously.

At first and cursorily, this suggestion may appear somewhat illogical,
for it is admittedly not logically consistent for a person to claim that
something exists at the same time that he denies its existence. We contend,
however, that actual death attitudes do not necessarily conform with the
basic canons of western logic and that, furthermore, continued exclusive
reliance upon traditional dictates of common sense logic contributes to
the perpetuation of ineffectual and unenlightened inquiry. For example,
the elementary rules of application for complementary terms may be
logically unassailable, but empirically inappropriate or vacuous: While
the statement, "All death attitudes are either acceptance or nonaccept-
ance," may be formally true by definition, it may be misleading and quite
erroneous in light of empirical evidence.[1] Indeed, enlightened contemporary scientists are coming ever more to appreciate the fact that the
traditional classificatory ("either/or") and quantitative ("more or less")
fundamentals of our system of logic may not always be applicable to the
description and explanation of a world that is not necessarily bound by
man's logic. We are finding increasingly that

...the more we penetrate into our knowledge of the universe, the more we are aware of the fact that the meanings of life are too large to be exclusive and that we must employ multiple explanations to begin to adequately interpret the phenomena that are experienced in existence. The 'both-ands' have acquired a new level of scientific respectability.[2]

The occurrence and significance of these "both-ands" has been recognized in several areas of human behavior. Notably, psychologists have discovered that man is quite capable of action that is non-logical or non-rational, as is indicated by such important concepts as 'ambivalence' (holding two contradictory emotions, for example, love and hate), and the closely related notion of 'approach-avoidance conflict,' "...in which a person is both attracted and repelled by the same goal."[3] Interestingly, the concept of 'ambivalence' was originally suggested and considered seriously by Freud in his attempt to explain the relationship of the living toward their dead relatives. The bereaved mourn the dead because of their love for the person in life, yet, they simultaneously rejoice in his death, since it brings to an end many of the problems the deceased had presented while alive.[4] The concept of ambivalence seems to be related or applicable to so much of human behavior that some psychologists have claimed that no one is free of ambivalent feelings, and "...that there is a streak of ambivalence in all our personal relations..."[5]

A phenomenon analogous to ambivalence characterizes American death attitudes. Individual Americans seem to possess contradictory attitudes toward their own deaths, and the culture of the United States appears to embody equally paradoxical attitudes toward death in general. Unfortunately, no direct evidence is yet available which might tend to confirm or infirm this thesis, since, as we have already indicated, previous research has generally proceeded out of a misformulation of the question in "either/or" terms. There exists sufficient indirect evidence in support of this twofold hypothesis, however, to suggest that it be entertained seriously and that research should be redirected in pursuit of its verification or refutation.[6] We present our rationale by considering first the cultural argument.

The cultural paradox

In the preceding chapter it was seen how the findings of anthropologists who studied preliterate societies revealed "the" attitudes and belief systems of their cultures to be characterized by homogeneity, consistency, and integration;[7] and how, as a consequence, there developed a natural propensity to assume that all cultures were so characterized.

Yet, even in the context of highly organized cultural complexes as regards most matters of human life, anthropologists were discovering that, with respect to death, some preliterate cultures lacked this homogeneity and consistency of attitudes. It seems, by virtue of these findings, that it is indeed possible for even a relatively simple culture to embody contradictory death attitudes, regardless of logical dictates to the contrary.

When Malinowski studied the funeral practices of the Melanesian culture, he found that contradictory attitudes were exhibited toward the dead, since in the funeral rites "...there was shown a desire to maintain the tie with the deceased and the parallel tendency to break the bond."[8] Corresponding contrary attitudes toward the ghosts of the dead are also commonly evidenced by preliterate cultures: While the deceased is viewed with love and it is believed that his ghost guides and protects living relatives, the same ghost is also regarded with fear, fear that it may return to life or attempt to summons the living to join him in the world of the spirits.[9] Opler has quite clearly and convincingly demonstrated such ambivalence in the funeral customs of the Apache culture, where

> ...Apache wail, tear their clothes, cut their hair, live purely, and shun social events to emphasize their grief and affection at the death of a relative, and yet by a hasty burial, destruction of all property that had come in contact with the deceased, demolishment of the home in which he had lived, refusal to allow his name to be uttered, fear of sickness induced by the return of his ghost or dreams in which he appears, etc., indicate a lively terror and apprehension in regard to the departed.[10]

In contrast to the preliterate culture, that of the United States is so markedly heterogeneous in virtually all of its attitudes, beliefs, and values, that it has been frequently said to lack a single, discernible culture. Within this highly diversified and complicated context, inconsistencies and contradictions flourish. For example, Americans embrace sociocultural mores which stress "getting ahead" and beating others, while at the same time they value cooperation and humanitarianism. "Thus, there emerges a frustrating conflict between competition and co-operation."[11] Other antagonisms exist between the Protestant work ethic and hedonism, between our pragmatism and our conceptions of morality, between equalitarianism and racism, between individual freedom and the emphasis upon conformity, and the like.[12] In light of these and numerous other intrinsic conflicts, the existence of contradictory attitudes especially as regards such an emotion-laden concern as death should certainly not be surprising.

It is not only highly likely that the cultural paradox should exist, but it may even be a virtual necessity, since the cultural maintenance of a pure or total attitude of either acceptance or denial would be suicidal, both for the culture and for the society. A society's culture could hardly be viewed as a credible source of values, norms, and beliefs if it embodied only an attitude of death denial. Furthermore, the total and uncompromising denial of death's reality would render the event of every individual's death a cause of utter chaos within the society, for its members would know neither how to react nor what to believe, and mass confusion as to the meaning and significance of the phenomenon would result. Similarly, a total cultural commitment to an attitude of death acceptance would also invite disaster, since

> it would lead either to mass suicide (since for a great part of mankind life is such a burden that the terror of death is probably an important factor in keeping it going) or to dissolution of all law and order...[13]

Thus, since a culture cannot survive while maintaining exclusively either an attitude of death acceptance or death denial, it is forced to maintain both simultaneously, regardless of the contradiction involved.

There is highly suggestive evidence from a variety of sources that such a cultural paradox does indeed characterize contemporary United States. For example, our culture does not possess a single or unitary meaning or connotation of death, but rather embodies numerous conceptions, both positive and negative, which have direct implications for both accepting and denying attitudes. Attached to death are such positive meanings and connotations as deliverance from unbearable situations (for example, from pain, old age, or debt), undisturbed sleep and a state of complete rest, reunion with loved ones, rebirth (rejuvenation and reincarnation), love and sexuality, and an ultimate triumph over the uncertainties of life. Some of death's negative aspects include separation from cherished persons and things, loss (in many ways, such as loss of pleasures of the body), trauma (catastrophic or malevolent death), punishment, masochism, and mass destruction.[14] It may be that the cultural embodiment of contrary attitudes necessitates the positive and negative meanings of death, or that the positive and negative meanings demand the contradictory attitudes, each being necessary to cope with the other; but which causes which is not important. What *is* important is that the existence of one most certainly implies the existence of the other. Feifel similarly implies a state of cultural contradiction when he argues cogently that

> ...Profound contradictions exist in our thinking about death. Our tradition assumes that 'man is both terminated by death and capable of continuing in some other sense beyond death.' Death is viewed on the one hand as a 'wall,' the

ultimate personal disaster, and suicide as an act of a sick mind; on the other, death is regarded as a 'doorway,' a point in time on the way to eternity.[15]

Those who must continually deal with death would naturally be expected to feel and show signs of the pressure inherent in treating the dead in accordance with such contradictory attitudes and traditions. Fulton and Geis have contended that the funeral director, for example, "...is caught between ambivalent demands...," because our culture prescribes that he must hide the reality of death to protect those who are not emotionally strong enough to cope with it, while at the same time it dictates that he call attention to the corpse so that the fact of death might be grasped.[16] As a direct consequence of these quite incompatible expectations, the funeral director, "...both blunts and sharpens the reality of death."

Further evidence suggestive of the American culture's simultaneous acceptance and denial of death is provided by reference to the traditional taboo on death conversation. In particular, the characteristic avoidance of discussions of the topic may be due neither to indifference nor even to denial of death *per se,* but rather to the inevitable conflict generated by the cultural contradictions. In line with this contention, Parsons has reminded us that studies of voting behavior have revealed that "apathy" in election campaigns (which can be observed in such behavior as the lack of discussion about candidates and issues, or in the failure to vote) is not ordinarily attributable to indifference, as might be expected, but rather to the existence of a state of conflict within the individual caused by contradictions or "cross pressures" forced upon him by the external situation. Presumably, "...it may therefore very well be that some of our tendency to be silent about problems of the meaning of death is related to phenomena of conflict."[17]

The death attitudes embodied by a culture are, of course, manifested in many different ways–by the burial customs of the society, the language (euphemisms) used in connection with death, and the nature of and names attached to related societal practices. In this regard, it is illuminating to recall our discussions of Chapters Three and Four, where it became apparent that many of the very same customs and practices could be and were, in fact, used to bolster either the acceptance or the denial argument. The fact that so many of these customs and practices have been found to exhibit elements of both acceptance and denial provides further suggestive evidence for our contention that the culture of the United States does indeed embody both attitudes simultaneously.[18]

Additional support for our hypothesis may be derived from a consideration of certain fundamental historical realities. In particular, a distinguishing characteristic of the culture of the United States lies in the absence of anything which might be described as a single "genesis." Quite to the contrary, this culture is almost unique in the extent to which diffusion has functioned in its creation, the result of a history of relatively heterogeneous and heavy migration. It would be highly probable, therefore, that the cultural conglomerate emerging from this extensive borrowing of traits, values, beliefs, and attitudes would exhibit markedly dissimilar and even contradictory attitudes toward death. Similarly, throughout the history of this society, many individuals and a substantial number of different groups, especially religious groups, have acted as powerful forces in encouraging the adoption of new attitudes by the culture. Since preexisting conceptions and orientations have a way of persisting tenaciously even in the face of significant change, attitudes of acceptance and denial could easily have developed in antagonistic coexistence.

Historically, the culture of the United States has also nurtured the evolution of a scientific-rational orientation. While prehistoric and preliterate man tended to see life in all things, even in rocks and trees, with the result that death was an "unthinkable anomaly," the cultural theme of scientism and rationalism provides an antithetical world view, since "...amid dead matter, life seems an unaccountable, brief flash in the interstellar dark."[19] Through its reversal of the idea that so much of our environment is filled with living spirits, the scientific-rational orientation has rendered death more consistent with our world view, thus making it easier to accept. At the same time, however, we have retained our conceptions of motion, viewing the world in terms of clashing forces, dialectical processes, causality, continuous and ubiquitous change, and "progress." Consequently, death, which represents a state of eternal rest and motionlessness, is ultimately incomprehensible and must be denied.

The demographic realities of our more recent history call, too, for both cultural acceptance and denial of death. As we have seen, death has become increasingly confined to the aged, a situation that is mixed in its effects upon death attitudes. On the one hand, as Parsons has argued, the fact that death is becoming primarily restricted to old age makes it appear a natural and inevitable conclusion of a long life.[20] This tendency, of course, lends itself readily to attitudinal acceptance. On the other hand, however, this very concentration of death among the aged prompts the vast majority of Americans, who are well below the "elderly" level, to conceive of death as an event of the distant future, one not, to be entertained seriously for the present. Contrary to Parsons' implications then, an attitude of death denial is also implied.

In addition to all of the factors considered thus far, it is important to recognize that the death attitudes embodied by the culture of the United

States must be responsive to the needs and nature of the American people, a people who take pride in their realism, their pragmatism, and their ability to live without self-delusion. Indeed, they have probably become even more realistic in recent years, and many have exhibited the desire to rid themselves of what they consider to be "crutches" in dealing with death, thereby revealing an increasing propensity toward death acceptance. The traditional belief in an afterlife has often been regarded as such a "crutch;" together with other such beliefs, "Those old religious assurances that there would be a gathering-in someday have largely been discarded..."[21] As a consequence of the passing of such beliefs, however, these people have been left more apprehensive about death, and have found it necessary to deny its existence in an attempt to alleviate the fear. Paradoxically, then, the American's realistic acceptance of death entails the abandonment of "crutches," which brings about a greater fear, and thus denial, of death. In light of these contradictions, and in order to be responsive to the needs and nature of the American people, the death attitudes embodied and maintained by the culture of the United States can only be contradictory.

A final suggestion is based upon a recognition of the fact that modern America exists under the constant threat of nuclear annihilation, which would mean death, not only for individual Americans, but also for the whole society and its culture. This threat forces acceptance of death: One is not only constantly reminded that a barrage of missiles could at any moment snuff out his life, but also is allowed no delusions of invincibility, for his human frailty is made all too clear by the awesome destructive powers of nuclear weaponry. Yet, as Morgenthau reminds us, this same threat increases denial of death. The possibility of nuclear war, he says, not only destroys man's faith in a social immortality by removing all monuments to, and signs of, man's existence, but it also robs his death of all potential significance, since he cannot even die of his own volition for a cause, a belief, his family's honor or protection, or for a better world. Again, the cultural embodiment of death attitudes must cope with a reality which demands both acceptance and denial of death.

Our discussion thus far has hopefully revealed that there are in fact a number of persuasive indications that, despite the logical inconsistency, the culture of contemporary United States does, and indeed must, simultaneously embody attitudes of both acceptance and denial. One final question deserves a well-reasoned answer, however: in light of these cultural contradictions, and in light of all the other realities of life and death in this society, how do the majority of individual Americans view their own deaths? The following section addresses itself to this most important query.

The individual response

As we have already indicated at the beginning of this chapter, we are hypothesizing that individual Americans, like the culture which they share, accept death as inevitable and real yet simultaneously hold attitudes of staunch denial. Unfortunately, once again we observe that there exist no definitive studies conducted specifically as tests of this hypothesis, since previous research has been designed so as to discover either acceptance or denial, thereby precluding the revelation of both. Consequently, we must again look to more indirectly related research in our preliminary efforts to validate our contention.

We have previously pointed out that the individual American receives very little guidance in forming his attitudes toward death, either from his parents or from his society, and that the particular nature of his resultant attitudes is quite dependent upon his own individual experiences with death and death-related events and issues It should be immediately obvious that such experiences are never totally positive nor totally negative, but rather highly varied and even contradictory in their effects and implications. For example, a child's pet dog dies and the child is thereby provided with a negative death connotation which might generalize readily to his attitudes toward his own death. A few weeks later, this same child gets lost in the woods near his home; he is eventually found by his parents who tell him anxiously that they were afraid he had died, that they cried at the thought, and worried about him all night. In light of his parents' increased attention and concern, the child attaches a positive connotation to being dead. Since one's experiences are so mixed in their implications, it seems entirely reasonable to suppose that attitudes of both acceptance and denial might well develop in all or most Americans.

A second factor which we have previously observed to have important consequences for the development of death attitudes is the individual's emotional response to death. On the one hand, we have seen that the fear of death, an emotion which lends itself readily to attitudes of denial, is virtually universal. On the other hand, however, the death wish seems nearly as universal as the fear of death; this response makes death attractive and prompts its acceptance. Since both the fear of death and the death wish constitute an intrinsic part of our beings, we are thus emotionally predisposed, in fact, compelled, to accept and deny death simultaneously.

Our hypothesis finds further indirect support in the argument that our view of an afterlife (and, by association, death) is conditioned by, or results from, our attitudes toward our parents, attitudes which are most certainly contradictory.

...The fundamental situation is the ambivalence of the fear of parents' power to inflict death and the need of the parents' protection. Both are projected as the wrathful and merciful deity, and to immortality as hell and heaven. Because of the ambivalence, the religious solution is not a solution; it provides protection, but it also perpetuates the parents.[22]

Even if contrary attitudes toward parents are irrelevant in the present context, the ambivalence toward an afterlife remains a determining factor, since there purportedly exists both a heaven and a hell. One reacts emotionally to heaven in a positive way and accepts his own death because heaven promises eternal bliss; yet hell is also a possibility, evoking negative emotions which compel one to deny death's threat of eternal damnation.

Before proceeding further with the development of the rationale for our argument, it should prove both illuminating and fruitful to elaborate upon our original hypothesis by considering more specifically the precise form assumed by this state of contradiction in death attitudes within the individual. In particular, it is our contention that *reason and emotion conflict in this regard.* That is, *on a conscious, intellectual level the individual accepts his death, while on a generally unconscious, emotional plane he denies it.* Let us now probe more deeply in an attempt to discern why this should be the case.

From a very early age, and throughout our lives, we learn of numerous deaths in the course of casual conversation and through the mass media, and we occassionally witness the deaths of friends and relatives. In due course, our intellect becomes unquestionably aware that all men must die; we become conscious of the fact that death constitutes a necessary component of the human scene. Since we also know that we are men, we are intellectually compelled to accept death as inevitable and real. At some time in our lives, then, we consciously apply a modified form of the traditional example of a logically correct syllogism to ourselves:

All men are mortal
I am a man–
therefore,
I must die

So compelling is this intellectual acceptance of death that it perhaps constitutes the single most strongly held individual attitude. Unlike almost any other belief, the certain knowledge of death's inevitability is not derived from nor dependent upon other beliefs held by the individual. Furthermore, it is supported by everyone, and taken for granted by all men as a given premise of human existence. Consequently, the intellectual attitudinal acceptance of death is never challenged. If a person's belief that his death is inevitable were somehow successfully disputed, he would probably begin to doubt all of his other beliefs, including who he was.

Running contrary to this conscious, intellectual acceptance of death is the unconscious, emotional denial. As we have already noted, death means separation, both from loved ones and from worldly pleasures; a cessation of the physical self; implied failure; the possibility of eternal damnation; and the like. All of these are emotionally unacceptable eventualities and must be denied. Even more important in the present context is the fact that, while the individual "knows" he must die, he is emotionally compelled to deny the reality of his death, for he is quite unable to imagine himself as being dead. Epicurus was one of the earliest Western thinkers to comment upon the fact that death is unimaginable to the individual, when he maintained that, "When I am, death is not... When death is, I am not. Therefore, we can never have anything to do with death."[23] As Freud has similarly indicated, man in his subconscious thoughts cannot conceive of himself as anything but immortal, regardless of the intellectual dictates of his conscious mind, and

> Much has been altered, or at least ought to have been altered, in our thinking about death by Freud's terse dictum: the unconscious is immortal... The sense of immortality cannot be irradicated, either by rational argument or by experience of the death of others, since man cannot have an inner awareness of a world in which he himself would not be the central point of reference.[24]

One attempts to imagine himself dead, perhaps in a casket surrounded by flowers, but his subconscious will not let him truly feel this death; while his mirror image lies in the casket, his deepest self stands outside of it, an interested spectator. What seems to be evident here is the dichotomy involved between the way the individual views himself both as subject and as object:

> Whatever attempt he makes to project himself into the time of death, it results only in seeing the *other one,* an object, not the *subjective one,* the 'I' of the here and now. A phantasy, absolute subjective death is impossible to imagine.[25]

Thus, we observe that man contains within himself a most profound contradiction. At the conscious, intellectual level he is absolutely convinced that he must die, this belief being reinforced and sustained by contacts with those around him who share it, as well as by the knowledge of the deaths of others. He can be more certain of his death than of his name. His unconscious is "immortal," however, denying the reality of his death and not allowing him to imagine himself dead. There is absolutely no way to eradicate this emotional feeling of immortality, so that the individual's emotions deny his death quite as steadfastly as his intellect affirms it. The unconscious response allows him to conceive of himself dying only as object, with the real "I" looking on, and even at that, personal death, "...can be imagined only with a considerable degree of distance, blurring, and denial..."[26]

Robert Lifton has discussed two conceptions which shed further light on the total inability of the unconscious to feel death, and the concomitant necessity for an attitude of denial.[27] While Lifton employs these notions in another context, the reader should quickly appreciate their relevance to our topic of concern. The first such concept is that in which death is conceived as the "severance of the sense of connection" between man and the various segments of his world, including people and things. Since such a sense of attachment is necessary to continuity and relatedness, the deepest unconscious part of the self demands a denial of the death which is "...a test of this sense of connection in that it threatens us with that which is most intolerable: *total* severance."[28] Undoubtedly, one would find "total severance" from his world not only intolerable, but also quite inconceivable, with the self thereby connected or related to nothing. The unconscious would similarly rebel against imaginary death and call for an attitude of denial because of the sense we all have of "...movement, of development, and change...," reflected in such truisms as "The world is in flux," "Change is inevitable," and "You never step into the same river twice;" in a philosophy such as Hegel's dialectic; or in Marx's social-philosophical theory of history and social change. Death is, of course, the direct antithesis of movement, and it is doubtful whether we are capable of envisioning such non-movement or of accepting emotionally the possibility of finding ourselves in such a state. Our perceptual systems are characterized by such a strong and salient sense of movement, that it is virtually impossible to conceive of a completely unchanging and eternally stagnant state such as death. If the reader doubts this contention, he is asked to think of the most immovable object possible. Once it is pictured in the mind, even this object can be visualized as moving.

Further and still more persuasive preliminary support for the acceptance-denial hypothesis as applied to individuals is provided by reference to the fact that different measurement techniques have characteristically revealed different attitudes. One investigator studies a group of subjects, employing overt questioning procedures to reveal attitudes operating at the conscious, intellectual level of awareness, and finds that the group exhibits attitudinal acceptance; a second studies a comparable group, using a more covert projective technique to tap the emotional, unconscious plane, and discovers that the individuals in his group evidence death denial. Alexander and Alderstein have shown clearly that projective measurement techniques yield findings which may directly contradict verbal level tests. In accord with our hypothesis, their observation implies that attitudes toward death operate on at least two, more or less distinct, levels of consciousness:

> It is suggested that in view of the discrepancy between these results and others using the questionnaire and interview techniques, and in view of the significant differences in individual responses found in the study, there may be two levels of functioning in the human organism when dealing with the problem of death.[29]

The notion of multilevel functioning of death attitudes also finds support in the findings of certain studies dealing with the fear of death. While few people reveal death anxiety on the "verbal conscious level," the thought of death has been found to provoke fear on the "non-verbal or unconscious level."[30]

At least two other factors may be cited as indicating the likelihood of simultaneous individual acceptance and denial of death. The first of these is Rheingold's conception of the "distance factor," analogous to our notion of the "subjective time factor," which suggests

> ...a contradiction in the attitudes toward death. On the one hand, in reality and because of the idea of punitive destruction, we may be struck down in the next moment. On the other, the delusion of invulnerability creates infinite distance.[31]

This distance factor is clearly consistent with our hypothesis. On the intellectual-conscious level we accept death, since we are cognizant of "reality" and are therefore reminded that at any moment "we may be struck down." The unconscious-emotional level does not allow us to "feel" death, however, and it thereby provides a "delusion of invulnerability" which compels us to deny death by conceptualizing it as infinitely distant.

Finally, Carl Jung alluded to our hypothesis when he maintained that "Many young people have at the bottom a panic-fear of life (though at the same time they intensely desire it)..."[32] Whether young, old, or in between, none of our lives are either trouble free or worthless. Consequently, ambivalence toward life is an inevitable aspect of the human condition. Since the way we feel about life is mirrored in the way we feel about death, ambivalence toward death is the inexorable accompaniment of ambivalence toward life: The individual is thereby predisposed to attitudes of both acceptance and denial of death.

Conclusion

In light of the preliminary and indirect evidence which we have considered, it is reasonable to conclude tentatively that the majority of individuals in contemporary United States feel, as did the respondent of a very early study, that

> My death is probable, but only in a dim, distant fashion... I reason that my death is not only probable, but certain, but my imagination fails to picture such an event except in a crude fashion which is forced and artificial.[33]

The inevitable consequence of this apparently perennial contradiction between the individual's rational recognition of the inevitability of death and his concomitant inability to feel death's reality seems indeed to be the simultaneous maintenance of attitudes of acceptance and denial. This individual response to death is also entirely consistent with the cultural paradox concerning death attitudes. We have observed that, with regard to both the culture and the individual, previous research has typically proceeded from the assumption that there must exist *an* attitude of *either* acceptance *or* denial of death. We are contending here that this oversimplistic "either/or" variety of thinking on the topic of American attitudes toward death has been stifling to definitive and conclusive findings in the area.

If we are ever to achieve an adequate understanding of the complex and multifaceted phenomenon of death attitude formation, structure, and change, our discussion suggests at least two major reorientations in general strategy.[34] First, rather than being conducted in a fashion which will stimulate the revelation of but one attitude or the other, research should be designed and executed so as to allow the discovery of *varying degrees* of *acceptance,* or of *denial,* or of *both.* Secondly, multilevel analysis should be rigorously employed to uncover attitudes operating at both the intellectual-conscious and emotional-unconscious levels. Practically speaking, this means the simultaneous implementation of a wide variety and substantial number of both overt and covert measurement techniques, which would not only make possible the careful exploration of attitudes operating at various levels of awareness, but which might also provide a series of cross-checks for the purpose of ensuring instrument validity and reliability. As Rheingold has concluded: "Of the several [methodological] requirements, multilevel analysis seems to be the most important. Attitudes are both conscious and unconscious..."[35]

The shift in emphasis which we are urging should also prove favorable to a better understanding of culture, for the cultural embodiment of attitudes of acceptance and denial provides sociologists with a fascinating opportunity to investigate the dynamics of a culture simultaneously maintaining contradictory attitudes, the processes by which it deals with the accompanying conflicts, how it integrates contrary views, and how these numerous and antagonistic attitudes are translated into concrete behavior of individuals and groups.

As the preceding discussion has implied, the acceptance-denial controversy has embraced three levels of reality: the cultural, the societal, and the individual. The methodological problems discussed in Chapter Five moved us closer to a resolution on all three levels by dramatizing the extent to which the inconsistent and contradictory findings have been exacerbated or magnified by numerous methodological inadequacies. Chapter Six provided a resolution to the controversy at the societal level by attempting to demonstrate that no "societal" attitude exists. Finally, the arguments and rationale of this chapter have been presented in an attempt to resolve the controversy at both the cultural and individual levels, by suggesting cultural and individual simultaneous acceptance and denial of death.

Hopefully, we have now laid the acceptance-denial controversy to rest. Of course, we feel ambivalent toward its death. We are sorry to witness the passing of the controversy, for it has provided us with intellectual challenge and excitement, and we do not part easily with something with which we have lived and worked and toward which we have developed strong emotional attachments. Simultaneously, however, we are pleased at the death of the controversy, for it has functioned to preclude sound inquiry into and knowledge of American death attitudes for too long a time. As Garrett Hardin has observed, "However much we may enjoy controversies—and sometimes they are great fun—we hope ultimately to bring each controversy to a close."[36] Pending the fruits of more enlightened and rigorous research, which we ourselves intend to pursue, we leave the reader to ponder the implications of the following observation:

> Socrates... died in good cheer and in control, unlike the agony of Jesus with his deep human cry of desertion and loneliness. Americans tend to behave as Socrates did. But there is more of what Jesus stands for lurking in our unconscious...[37]

NOTES

1. For an elementary discussion concerning complementary terms, see, for example, T. Vernon and L. Nissen, *Reflective Thinking: The Fundamentals of Logic,* Belmont, California: Wadsworth Publishing Company, 1968, p. 94.

2. E. N. Jackson, "Grief and Religion," in Herman Feifel (ed.), *The Meaning of Death,* New York: McGraw-Hill Book Company, Inc., 1959, p. 218.

3. G. Lehner and E. Kube, *The Dynamics of Personal Adjustment,* Englewood Cliffs, N. J.: Prentice-Hall, Inc., 1964, p. 99.

4. S. Freud, *Totem and Taboo,* New York: Moffat, Yard and Company, 1918, p. 105.

5. H. Becker and D. K. Bruner, "Attitudes Toward Death and the Dead and Some Possible Causes of Ghost Fear," *Mental Hygiene,* 1931, 15, p. 833.

6. It is interesting to note that our formulation of this twofold hypothesis of cultural and individual simultaneous acceptance and denial is consistent with the recommendations discussed in R. Bendix and B. Berger, "Images of Society and Problems of Concept Formation in Sociology," in Llewellyn Gross (ed.), *Symposium on Sociological Theory,* New York: Harper and Row, Publishers, 1959, pp. 92-118. Specifically, Bendix and Berger point to the programmatic utility of what they label 'the perspective of dual tendencies,' which involves the recognition of "...tendencies or forces which are linked and opposite at the same time..." As the authors have indicated clearly,

    The frequent formulation of paired concepts in sociology may be seen as an intellectual response to the 'perspective of dual tendencies' ...We believe that the empirical foundation of this perspective lies in the fact that concrete human relationships are ambiguous, and that this amibiguity is manifest in social action and its consequences. This is another way of saying [for example] that mankind is neither entirely dependent nor entirely free, that social interaction is partly communicative and partly competitive, that *both* the I and the Me participate in every social transaction, and so forth. This insight, however, is often lost somewhere between the point at which concepts are formulated and the point at which testable hypotheses are developed (*ibid.,* p. 99).

7. The notions of homogeneity, consistency, and integration, of course, constitute some of the central assumptions of early functionalism in anthropology and sociology. For a discussion of some of the deficiencies involved in reliance upon these and related assumptions, see, for example, R. K. Merton, *Social Theory and Social Structure,* New York: The Free Press, 1968, pp. 73-138.

8. D. G. Mandelbaum, "Social Uses of Funeral Rites," in Feifel, *op. cit.,* pp. 208-209.

9. R. Blauner, "Death and the Social Structure," *Psychiatry,* 1966, 29, p. 382.

10. Lehner and Kube, *op. cit.,* p. 96.

11. *Ibid.,* p. 96.

12. For an interesting discussion of major American cultural themes and some of their inherent contradictions and compatibilities, see J. Biesanz and M. Biesanz, *Introduction to Sociology,* Englewood Cliffs, N. J.: Prentice-Hall, Inc., 1969, pp. 84-89; and R. M. Williams, Jr., *American Society: A Sociological Interpretation* (second edition), New York: Alfred A. Knopf, Inc., 1960, especially Chs. XI and XIV.

13. H. Marcuse, "The Ideology of Death," in Feifel, *op. cit.,* p. 70.

14. J. C. Rheingold, *The Mother, Anxiety and Death,* Boston: Little, Brown and Company, 1967, pp. 11-21.

15. Feifel, *op. cit.,* XIV.

16. R. Fulton and G. Geis, "Death and Social Values," in Robert Fulton (ed.), *Death and Identity,* New York: John Wiley and Sons, Inc., p. 72.

17. T. Parsons, "Death in American Society: A Brief Working Paper," *American Behavioral Scientist,* 1963, 6, p. 63.

18. It is tempting here to pursue this point by analyzing each of the practices previously noted in an attempt to demonstrate how each reflects both acceptance and denial. Unfortunately, however, this procedure would be quite unacceptable, since it would involve the use of the contradictory findings to support an hypothesis which is purported to explain these same contradictions.

19. "On Death as a Constant Companion," *Time Magazine,* November 12, 1965, p. 53.

20. Parsons, *op. cit.,* pp. 61-62.

21. "On Death as a Constant Companion," *op. cit.,* p. 53.

22. Rheingold, *op. cit.,* p. 45.

23. From "On Death as a Constant Companion," *op. cit.,* p. 52.

24. F. Borkenau, "The Concept of Death," *The Twentieth Century,* 1955, 157, p. 313.

25. A. D. Weisman and T. P. Hackett, "Predilection to Death," in Fulton, *op. cit.,* p. 317.

26. R. J. Lifton, "On Death and Death Symbolism: The Hiroshima Disaster, *American Scholar,* 1965. 34, p. 266.

27. *Ibid.,* pp. 257-272.

28. *Ibid.,* p. 267.

29. I. E. Alexander and A. M. Alderstein, "Death and Religion," in Feifel, *op. cit.,* p. 283.

30. R. L. Fulton, "Introduction: Attitudes and Responses toward Death," in Fulton, *op. cit.,* p. 81.

31. Rheingold, *op. cit.,* p. 40.

32. C. G. Jung, "The Soul and Death," (1934) in Feifel, *op. cit.,* p. 4.

33. W. Bromberg and P. Schilder, "Death and Dying," *Psychoanalytic Review,* 1933, 20, p. 143.

34. Further major and minor remedial changes are implicit in our discussion of methodology in Chapter Five.

35. Rheingold, *op. cit.,* p. 33.

36. G. Hardin, *Science and Controversy,* San Francisco: W. H. Freeman and Company, 1969, p. 2.

37. "On Death as a Constant Companion," *op. cit.,* p. 53.

References and Suggestions
for Further Reading

Alderstein, A. M., *The Relationship Between Religious Belief and Death Affect,* Unpublished Doctoral Dissertation, Princeton University, 1958.

Alexander, I. E. and A. M. Alderstein, "Affective Responses to the Concept of Death in a Population of Children and Early Adolescents," *Journal of Genetic Psychology,* 1958, 93, pp. 167-177.

— and —, "Death and Religion," in Herman Feifel (ed.), *The Meaning of Death,* New York: McGraw-Hill Book Company, Inc., 1959, pp. 271-283.

—, R. S. Colley, and A. M. Alderstein, "Is Death a Matter of Indifference?" *Journal of Psychology,* 1957, 43, pp. 277-283.

Alleman, S. A., "The Structure and Content of Belief Systems," *Dissertation Abstracts,* 1964, XXIV, p. 5536.

Anthony, S., *The Child's Discovery of Death,* New York: Harcourt, Brace and Company, 1940.

Becker, H., "The Sorrow of Bereavement," *Journal of Abnormal and Social Psychology,* 1933, 27, pp. 391-410.

— and D. K. Bruner, "Attitudes Toward Death and the Dead and Some Possible Causes of Ghost Fear," *Mental Hygiene,* 1931, 15, pp. 828-837.

Bender, L., *Aggression, Hostility and Anxiety in Children,* Springfield, Ill.: C. C. Thomas, 1953.

Bendix, R. and B. Berger, "Images of Society and Problems of Concept Formation in Sociology," in Llewellyn Gross (ed.), *Symposium on Sociological Theory,* New York: Harper and Row, Publishers, 1959, pp. 92-118.

Biesanz, J. and M. Biesanz, *Introduction to Sociology,* Englewood Cliffs, N. J.: Prentice-Hall, Inc., 1969.

Blauner, R., "Death and the Social Structure," *Psychiatry,* 1966, 29, pp. 378-394.

Bluestone, H. and C. C. McGahee, "Reaction to Extreme Stress: Impending Death by Execution," *American Journal of Psychiatry,* 1962, 119, pp. 393-396.

Borkenau, F., "The Concept of Death," *The Twentieth Century,* 1955, 157, pp. 313-329.

Bowman, L. *The American Funeral: A Study in Guilt, Extravagence, and Sublimity,* Washington, D. C.: Public Affairs Press, 1959.

Bromberg, W. and P. Schilder, "Death and Dying," *Psychoanalytic Review,* 1933, 20, pp. 133-185.

Butler, R. N., "The Life Review: An Interpretation of Reminiscence in the Aged," *Psychiatry,* 1963, 26, pp. 65-76.

Carmichael, B., "The Death Wish in Daily Life," *Psychoanalytic Review,* 1943, 30, pp. 59-66.

Carnell, E. J., "Fear of Death," *Christian Century,* 1963, 80, pp. 136-137.

Chadwick, M., "Notes Upon the Fear of Death," *International Journal of Psychoanalysis,* 1929, 10, pp. 321-334.

Choron, J., *Death and Western Thought,* New York: Collier-Macmillan Company, 1963.

—, *Modern Man and Morality,* New York: The MacMillan Company, 1964.

Christ, A. E., "Attitudes Toward Death Among a Group of Acute Geriatric Psychiatric Patients," *Journal of Gerontology*, 1961, 16, pp. 56-59.

Cleghorn, S., "Changing Thoughts of Death," *Atlantic Monthly*, 1923, 132, pp. 808-812.

Corey, L. G., "An Analogue of Resistance to Death Awareness," *Journal of Gerontology*, 1961, 16, pp. 59-60.

Cousinet, R., "L'Idée de la Mort chez les Enfants (The Idea of Death in Children)," *Journal of Normal and Pathological Psychology*, 1939, 36, pp. 65-75.

Davids, A., "Intolerance of Ambiguity," in Milton Waldman (ed.), *America Conquers Death*, New York: W. E. Rudge, 1928, pp. 161-177.

—, "Death by the Seven Year Old," *State Government*, 1940, 13, p. 209.

Diggory, J. C. and D. Z. Rothman, "Values Destroyed by Death," *Journal of Abnormal and Social Psychology*, 1961, 63, pp. 205-210.

Driver, C. "The Great Unmentionable," *Atlas*, August, 1965, 10, pp. 113-114.

Dumont, R. G. and W. J. Wilson, "Aspects of Concept Formation, Explication and Theory Construction in Sociology," *American Sociological Review*, 1967, 32, pp. 985-995.

Eissler, K. R., *The Psychiatrist and the Dying Patient*, New York, International University Press, 1955.

Eliot, T. D., "The Adjustive Behavior of Bereaved Families: A New Field for Research," *Social Forces*, 1930, 8, pp. 543-549.

—, "Bereavement as a Problem for Family Research and Technique," *The Family*, 1930, 11, pp. 114-115.

—, "A Step Toward the Social Psychology of Bereavement," *Journal of Abnormal and Social Psychology*, 1933, 27, pp. 380-390.

Faunce, W. A. and R. L. Fulton, "The Sociology of Death: A Neglected Area of Research," *Social Forces*, 1958, 36, pp. 205-209.

Feifel, H., "Attitudes Toward Death in Some Normal and Mentally Ill Populations," in Herman Feifel (ed.), *The Meaning of Death*, New York: McGraw-Hill Book Company, Inc., 1959, pp. 114-130.

—, *The Meaning of Death*, New York: McGraw-Hill Book Company, Inc., 1959.

—, "Death," *The Encyclopedia of Mental Health*, 1963, Vol. 2, pp. 427-450.

—, "Death," in Norman L. Farberow (ed.), *Taboo Topics*, New York: Atherton Press, 1963, pp. 8-21.

—, "The Taboo on Death," *American Behavioral Scientist*, 1963, 6, pp. 66-67.

—, "Attitudes of Mentally Ill Patients Toward Death," in Robert L. Fulton (ed.), *Death and Identity*, New York: John Wiley and Sons, Inc., 1965, pp. 131-141.

Fenichel, O., "A Critique of the Death Instinct," in *The Collected Papers of Otto Fenichel*, New York: W. W. Norton and Company, 1953, Vol. I, pp. 363-372.

Foxe, A. N., "Critique of Freud's Concept of a Death Instinct," *Psychoanalytic Review*, 1943, 30, pp. 417-427.

Frazer, J. G., *The Fear of the Dead in Primitive Religion*, London: Macmillan, 1933.

Freud, S., "Mourning and Melancholia," in Sigmund Freud, *Collected Papers*, New York: Basic Books, 1959, Vol. 4, pp. 152-170.

—, *Totem and Taboo*, New York: Moffat, Yard and Company, 1918.

Fulton, R. L., "The Clergyman and the Funeral Director: A Study in Role Conflict," *Social Forces*, 1961, 39, pp. 317-323.

—, "Attitudes Toward Death: A Discussion," *Journal of Gerontology*, 1961, 16, pp. 63-65.

—, "Introduction: Attitudes and Responses toward Death," in Robert L. Fulton (ed.), *Death and Identity*, New York: John Wiley and Sons, Inc., 1965, pp. 79-82.

—, "The Sacred and the Secular: Attitudes of the American Public toward Death, Funerals, and Funeral Directors," in Robert L. Fulton (ed.), *Death and Identity*, New York: John Wiley and Sons, Inc., 1965, pp. 89-105.

—, *Death and Identity*, New York: John Wiley and Sons, Inc., 1965.

— and G. Geis, "Death and Social Values," in Robert L. Fulton (ed.), *Death and Identity*, New York; John Wiley and Sons, Inc., 1965, pp. 67-75.

Galdston, I., "Eros and Thanatos: A Critique and Elaboration of Freud's Death Wish," *American Journal of Psychoanalysis*, 1955, 15, pp. 123-134.

Geiringer, E., "Fear of Death," *Spectator*, August 8, 1952, 189, pp. 179-180.

Glaser, B. and A. L. Strauss, *Awareness of Dying: A Study of Social Interaction*, Chicago: Aldine Publishing Company, 1965.

— and —, "Temporal Aspects of Dying as a Non-Scheduled Status Passage," *American Journal of Sociology*, 1965, 71, pp. 48-59.

Gorer, G., *Death, Grief and Mourning*, New York: Doubleday, 1965.

Gottlieb, C., "Modern Art and Death," in Herman Feifel (ed.), *The Meaning of Death*, New York: McGraw-Hill Book Company, Inc., 1959, pp. 157-188.

Graham, J. B., "Acceptance of Death—Beginning of Life," *North Carolina Medical Journal*, 1963, 24, pp. 317-319.

Grayton, A. H., "Orpheus Myth in North America," *Journal of American Folklore*, 1935, 48, pp. 263-293.

Greenberger, E. S., "Fantasies of Women Confronting Death: A Study of Critically Ill Patients," Unpublished Doctoral Dissertation, Radcliffe College, 1961, summarized in Robert White (ed.), *The Study of Lives*, New York: Atherton Press, 1963, pp. 107-113.

Guralanik, D. B. (General Editor), *Webster's New World Dictionary—Comprehensive Reference Edition*, New York: The World Publishing Company, 1961.

Habenstein, R. W., "The Social Organization of Death," *International Encyclopedia of the Social Sciences*, 1968, Vol. IV, pp. 26-28.

Hampton, F. A., "Fear of Death," *Discovery*, 1922, 3, pp. 285-288.

Hardin, G., *Science and Controversy*, San Francisco: W. H. Freeman and Company, 1969.

Hinton, J., *Dying*, Baltimore: Penguin Books, 1964.

Hocking, W. E., *The Meaning of Immortality in Human Experience*, New York: Harpers, 1957.

Hoffman, F. J., "Mortality and Modern Literature," in Herman Feifel (ed.), *The Meaning of Death*, New York: McGraw-Hill Book Company, Inc., 1959, pp. 133-156.

Hoffman, F. and M. W. Brody, "The Symptom: Fear of Death," *Psychoanalytic Review*, 1957, 44, pp. 433-438.

Hooper, W. T., "Personal Values and Meaning of Future Time and Death Among College Students," *Dissertation Abstracts*, 1962, XXIII, p. 2965.

Hutschnecker, A. A., "Personality Factors in Dying Patients," in Herman Feifel (ed.), *The Meaning of Death*, New York: McGraw-Hill Book Company, Inc., 1959, pp. 237-250.

Jackson, E. N., "Grief and Religion," in Herman Feifel (ed.), *The Meaning of Death,* New York: McGraw-Hill Book Company, Inc., 1959, pp. 218-233.

Jeffers, F. C., C. R. Nichols, and C. Eisdorfer, "Attitudes of Older Persons Toward Death: A Preliminary Study," *Journal of Gerontology,* 1961, 16, pp. 53-56.

Jung, C. G., "The Soul and Death," in Herman Feifel (ed.), *The Meaning of Death,* New York: McGraw-Hill Book Company, Inc., 1959, pp. 3-15.

Kalish, R. A., "An Approach to the Study of Death Attitudes," *American Behavioral Scientist,* 1963, 6, pp. 68-70.

—, "Some Variables in Death Attitudes," *Journal of Social Psychology,* 1963, 59, pp. 137-145.

—, "Aged and the Dying Process: The Inevitable Decision," *Journal of Social Issues,* 1965, 21, pp. 87-96.

—, "Death and Bereavement: A Bibliography," *Journal of Human Relations,* 1965, 13, pp. 118-141.

Kaplan, A., *The Conduct of Inquiry: Methodology for Behavioral Science,* San Francisco: Chandler Publishing Company, 1964.

Kasper, A. M., "The Doctor and Death," in Herman Feifel (ed.), *The Meaning of Death,* New York: McGraw-Hill Book Company, Inc., 1959, pp. 259-270.

Kastenbaum, R., "Time and Death in Adolescence," in Herman Feifel (ed.), *The Meaning of Death,* New York: McGraw-Hill Book Company, Inc., 1959, pp. 99-113.

Kaufmann, W., "Existentialism and Death," in Herman Feifel (ed.), *The Meaning of Death,* New York: McGraw-Hill Book Company, Inc., 1959, pp. 39-63.

Kephart, W. M., "Status After Death," *American Sociological Review,* 1950, 15, pp. 635-643.

Kroeber, T. C., "The Coping Functions of the Ego Mechanisms," in Robert White (ed.), *The Study of Lives,* New York: Atherton Press, 1963.

Krupp, G. R. and B. Kligfeld, "The Bereavement Reaction: A Cross-cultural Evaluation," *Journal of Religion and Health,* 1962, 1, pp. 222-246.

Lehner, G. and E. Kube, *The Dynamics of Personal Adjustment,* Englewood Cliffs, N. J.: Prentice-Hall, Inc., 1964.

Leviton, D., "The Perceptual Defense of Amateur Sports Car Drivers and Bowlers to Death-Crash Word Stimuli," *Dissertation Abstracts,* 1967, XXVIII, pp. 2540a-2541a.

Lifton, R. J., "On Death and Death Symbolism: The Hiroshima Disaster," *American Scholar,* 1965, 34, pp. 257-272.

Lindemann, E., "Symptomatology and Management of Acute Grief," *American Journal of Psychiatry,* 1944, 101, pp. 141-148.

Lowry, R. J., "Male-Female Differences in Attitudes Toward Death," *Dissertation Abstracts,* 1965, XXVIII, pp. 1607b-1608b.

MacLaurin, H., "In the Hour of Their Going Forth," *Social Case Work,* 1959, 40, pp. 136-141.

Mahler, M. S., "Helping Children to Accept Death," *Child Study,* 1950, 27, pp. 98-99, 119-120.

Mandelbaum, D. G., "Social Uses of Funeral Rites," in Herman Feifel (ed.), *The Meaning of Death,* New York: McGraw-Hill Book Company, Inc., 1959, pp. 189-217.

Mannheim, K., *Ideology and Utopia,* New York: Harcourt, Brace and World, Inc., 1936.

Marcuse, H., "The Ideology of Death," in Herman Feifel (ed.), *The Meaning of Death,* New York: McGraw-Hill Book Company, Inc., 1959, pp. 64-76.

Martin, D. and L. S. Wrightsman, "The Relationship Between Religious Behavior and Concern About Death" *Journal of Social Psychology,* 1965, 65, pp. 317-323.

May, R., *Psychology and the Human Dilemma,* Princeton, N. J.: D. Van Nostrand Co., Inc., 1967.

McClelland, D. C., "The Harlequin Complex," in Robert White (ed.), *The Study of Lives,* New York: Atherton Press, 1963, pp. 94-119.

Means, M. H., "Fears of One Thousand College Women," *Journal of Abnormal and Social Psychology,* 1936, 31, pp. 291-311.

Meissner, W. W., "Affective Response to Psychoanalytic Death Symbols," *Journal of Abnormal and Social Psychology,* 1958, 56, pp. 295-299.

Merton, R. K., *Social Theory and Social Structure,* New York: The Free Press, 1968.

Mitchell, M. E., *The Child's Attitude Toward Death,* New York: Schocken Books, 1967.

Mitford, J., *The American Way of Death,* New York: Simon and Schuster, 1963.

Mitra, D. N., "Mourning Customs and Modern Life in Bengal," *American Journal of Sociology,* 1947, 52, pp. 309-311.

Monsour, K. J., "Asthma and the Fear of Death," *Psychoanalytic Quarterly,* 1960, 29, pp. 56-71.

Morgenthau, H. J., "Death in the Nuclear Age," *Commentary,* 1961, 32, pp. 231-239.

Murphy, G., "Discussion," in Herman Feifel (ed.), *The Meaning of Death,* New York: McGraw-Hill Book Company, Inc., 1959, pp. 317-340.

Myler, B. B., "Depression and Death in the Aged," *Dissertation Abstracts,* 1967, XXVIII, p. 2146.

Nagel, E., *The Structure of Science: Problems in the Logic of Scientific Explanation,* New York: Harcourt, Brace and World, Inc., 1961.

Nagy, M. H., "The Child's View of Death," in Herman Feifel (ed.), *The Meaning of Death,* New York: McGraw-Hill Book Company, Inc., 1959, pp. 79-98.

Neilson, G. S., "The Method of Self Confrontation," in Robert White (ed.), *The Study of Lives,* New York: Atherton Press, 1963, pp. 125-141.

Nettler, G., "Review Essay: On Death and Dying," *Social Problems,* 1967, 14, pp. 335-344.

"On Death as a Constant Companion," *Time Magazine,* November 12, 1965, pp. 52-54.

Opler, M. E., "Interpretation of Ambivalence of Two American Indian Tribes," *Journal of Social Psychology,* 1936, 7, pp. 82-116.

—, "Further Comparative Anthropological Data Bearing on the Solution of a Psychological Problem: Ambivalence in Respect to the Attitudes Connected with Death," *Journal of Social Psychology,* 1938, 9, pp. 477-483.

Owen, J. K., *Modern Concepts of Hospital Administration,* Philadelphia: Saunders, 1962.

Parsons, T., "Death in American Society: A Brief Working Paper," *American Behavioral Scientist,* 1963, 6, pp. 61-65.

Pound, L., "American Euphemisms for Dying, Death and Burial: An Anthology," *American Speech,* 1936, 11, pp. 195-202.

Rheingold, J. C., *The Mother, Anxiety and Death,* Boston: Little, Brown and Company, 1967.

Rhudick, P. J. and A. S. Dibner, "Age, Personality and Health Correlates of Death Concerns in Normal Aged Individuals," *Journal of Gerontology,* 1961, 16, pp. 44-49.

Riley, J. W., Jr., "Contemporary Society and the Institution of Life Insurance," *Journal of the American Society of Chartered Life Underwriters,* 1964, 18, No. 2, pp. 93-103.

—, "Death and Bereavement," *International Encyclopedia of the Social Sciences,* 1968, Vol. 4, pp. 19-25.

Rokeach, M., *Beliefs, Attitudes and Values,* San Francisco: Jossey-Bass, Inc., 1968.

Rosenthal, H., "The Fear of Death as an Indispensable Factor in Psychotherapy," *American Journal of Psychotherapy,* 1963, 17, pp. 619-630.

Ross, R. P., "Separation Fear and the Fear of Death in Children," *Dissertation Abstracts,* 1966, XXVII, pp. 2878b-2879b.

Russell, B., "Your Child and the Fear of Death," *The Forum,* 1929, 81, pp. 174-178.

Saul, L. J., "Reactions of a Man to Natural Death," *Psychoanalytic Quarterly,* 1959, 28, pp. 383-386.

Schilder, P. and D. Wechsler, "The Attitudes of Children Toward Death," *Pedagogical Seminary and the Journal of Genetic Psychology,* 1934, 45, pp. 406-451.

Schneider, L. and S. M. Dornbusch, *Popular Religion: Inspirational Books in America,* Chicago: University of Chicago Press, 1958.

Shneidman, E. S., "Orientations Toward Death: A Vital Aspect of the Study of Lives," in Robert White (ed.), *The Study of Lives,* New York: Atherton Press, 1963, pp. 201-227.

—, "The Enemy," *Psychology Today,* August, 1970, 4, pp. 37-41, 62-66.

—, "You and Death," *Psychology Today,* June, 1971, 5, pp. 43-45, 74-80.

—, and N. L. Faberow, "Suicide and Death," in Herman Feifel (ed.), *The Meaning of Death,* New York: McGraw-Hill Book Company, Inc., 1959, pp. 284-301.

Shrut, S. D., "Attitudes Toward Old Age and Death," *Mental Hygiene,* 1958, 42, pp. 259-266.

Spiro, M. E. (ed.), *Context and Meaning in Cultural Anthropology,* New York: The Free Press, 1965.

Stacey, C. L. and K. Marken, "The Attitudes of College Students and Penitentiary Inmates Toward Death and A Future Life," *Psychiatric Quarterly,* (Supplement), 1952, 26, pp. 27-32.

—, and M. L. Reichen, "Attitudes Toward Death and Future Life Among Normal and Subnormal Adolescent Girls," *Exceptional Children,* 1954, 20, pp. 259-262.

Steinzor, B., "Death and the Construction of Reality," in J. G. Peatman and

E. L. Hartley (eds.), *Festschrift for Gardner Murphy,* New York: Harper and Row, 1960, pp. 358-375.

Sudnow, D. N., "Passing On: The Social Organization of Dying in the County Hospital," *Dissertation Abstracts,* 1966, XXVIII, p. 834a.

—, *Passing On,* Englewood Cliffs, N. J.: Prentice-Hall, Inc., 1967.

Swenson, W. M., "Attitudes toward Death Among the Aged," in Robert Fulton (ed.), *Death and Identity,* New York: John Wiley and Sons, Inc., 1965, pp. 105-111.

—, "Attitudes Toward Death in an Aged Population," *Journal of Gerontology,* 1961, 16, pp. 49-52.

Taeuber, C. and I. B. Taeuber, *The Changing Population of the United States,* New York: John Wiley and Sons, Inc., 1958.

Tillich, P., "The Eternal Now," in Herman Feifel (ed.), *The Meaning of Death,* New York: McGraw-Hill Book Company, Inc., 1959, pp. 30-38.

Treanton, J., "A Discussion of a Symposium on Attitudes Toward Death in Older Persons," *Journal of Gerontology,* 1961, 16, p. 84.

United Nations, *Population Bulletin No. 6,* New York: United Nations, 1962.

Vernon, G. M., *Sociology of Death,* New York: The Ronald Press Company, 1970.

Vernon, T. and L. Nissen, *Reflective Thinking: The Fundamentals of Logic,* Belmont, California: Wadsworth Publishing Company, 1968.

Vital Statistics of the United States, 1967, Vol. II-"Mortality," Part B, Washington, D. C.: National Center for Health Statistics, 1969.

Volkart, E. H. and S. T. Michael, "Bereavement and Mental Health," in Robert Fulton (ed.), *Death and Identity,* New York: John Wiley and Sons, Inc. 1965, pp. 272-293.

Wahl, C. W., "The Fear of Death," in Robert Fulton (ed.), *Death and Identity,* New York: John Wiley and Sons, Inc., 1965, pp. 56-66.

Waldman, M., *America Conquers Death,* New York: W. E. Rudge, 1928.

Weisman, A. D. and T. P. Hackett, "Predilection to Death," in Robert Fulton (ed.), *Death and Identity,* New York: John Wiley and Sons, Inc., 1965, pp. 293-329.

White, R. W., *The Study of Lives,* New York: Atherton Press, 1963.

Williams, M., "Changing Attitudes Toward Death: A Survey of Contributions in Psychological Abstracts Over a Thirty Year Period," *Human Relations,* 1966, 19, pp. 405-423.

Williams, R. M., Jr., *American Society: A Sociological Interpretation* (second edition), New York: Alfred A. Knopf, Inc., 1960.

Wilson, W. J. and R. G. Dumont, "Rules of Correspondence and Sociological Concepts," *Sociology and Social Research,* 1968, 52, pp. 217-227.

Wittgenstein, G., "Fear of Dying and of Death as a Requirement of the Maturation Process in Man," *Hippokrates,* 1960, 31, pp. 765-769.

Zilboorg, G., "Fear of Death," *Psychoanalytic Quarterly,* 1943, 12, pp. 465-475.

1 2 3 4 5 6 7 8 9–RRD–79 78 77 76 75 74 73 72